Storie
to read
ud

Patrick Coghlan

50 Bible stories for assemblies, RE and all-age worship

In his role as an ordained Baptist minister, Patrick Coghlan has had many years' experience in using the Bible creatively in schools and all-age worship. A prolific and enthusiastic writer, he uses his material on a regular basis in his local primary schools and Baptist church, where he finds that his retelling of the Bible narratives gives plenty of opportunity to build up dialogue and promote discussion. His work has been approved by OFSTED with very positive results—especially about the opportunity to involve youngsters in discussion. His stories have been enjoyed by teachers, members of congregations, families and children themselves. Patrick is married with two children, aged 11 and 14, and enjoys writing all kinds of Christian resource material for adults and children alike, as well as writing short novels for children.

Acknowledgments

With grateful thanks to Neatishead County Primary School and Hoveton St John's County Primary School.

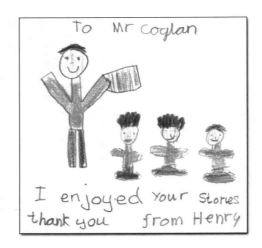

Text copyright © Patrick Coghlan 2004
Illustrations copyright © Baz Rowell 2004

The author asserts the moral right
to be identified as the author of this work

Published by
The Bible Reading Fellowship
First Floor, Elsfield Hall
15–17 Elsfield Way, Oxford OX2 8FG

ISBN 1 84101 362 5
First published 2004
10 9 8 7 6 5 4 3 2 1 0
All rights reserved

Acknowledgments
Unless otherwise stated, scripture quotations are taken from the Contemporary English Version of the Bible published by HarperCollins Publishers, copyright © 1991, 1992, 1995 American Bible Society.

A catalogue record for this book is available from the British Library

Printed and bound in Malta

Contents

Stories from the New Testament

Matthew's Gospel

The book of Acts

Introduction

Stories to read aloud is a selection of fifty Bible stories with related teaching resources, starting with Genesis and finishing with Acts. They are written for seven- to nine-year-olds in a descriptive and humorous style, ready to 'read aloud' in school assemblies, in the classroom or during all-age worship.

Teacher's information

Each chapter starts with a section containing a selection of flexible ideas to help the teacher develop the story around a framework of easy-to-prepare resources. The section contains:

 ### Bible reference

The Bible reference is given so that the leader can read the Bible passage from which the story is taken. Reading the original passage as part of the preparation for the session will help to give the teacher a full picture of how the session has been planned.

 ### Theme

The theme provides an at-a-glance summary of the core topic of the Bible passage.

 ### Key verse

A key verse from the Bible passage is given to help pinpoint the subject of the original biblical text.

 ### Talk about...

'Talk about' gives ideas for developing a related topic into a discussion.

 ### Aim

The aim of the session is given to clarify the teaching point and help identify learning outcomes.

Jigsaw puzzled

'Jigsaw puzzled' introduces the session with a relevant question addressed to God, with the intention of giving the children a focal point from which to spark ideas. The rest of the session seeks to find the answer to the question.

 ### Activitime

An activity is suggested for the group, which is linked with the theme in some way. It may be a group activity, something to be done individually, or a short drama. In every case, preparation is kept to the minimum.

 ### Jigsaw piece

One of the most difficult things about the Bible is trying to understand how everything fits together to form an overall picture—it's like making up a jigsaw puzzle. The jigsaw piece sets the individual story into context.

The story

 The story is the basis of the whole session and adheres closely to the original biblical text. It is hoped that as the stories are presented in a descriptive and humorous style, young people will be encouraged to read further Bible stories for themselves.

Prayback

This section is a prayer response and, in many ways, summarizes and concludes the whole session.

Stories from the Old Testament

The God of creation

Teacher's information

 Bible reference

The story is based on Genesis 1:1—2:4.

 Theme

God looks at everything that he has made and sees that it is very good.

 Key verse

God looked at what he had done. All of it was very good! Evening came and then morning—that was the sixth day.
GENESIS 1:31

 Talk about...

Something that we have taken a pride in making—maybe from the activities section.

 Aim

To recognize that God created the world and everything in it, including us, for a purpose.

Jigsaw puzzled

Dear God...
The world didn't just happen by mistake, did it?

 Activitime

Using a selection of felt-tips, glue, paper, cardboard tubes and so on, working individually or in groups, make something useful, beautiful, or both.

 Jigsaw piece

We cannot possibly imagine what things were like before the earth, our solar system and the universe beyond were created. Whatever it was like, God was present—he has always been. The Bible takes us back to this point of time, and shows us God the creator at work.

Prayback

God who made the world,
We thank you that you planned and made the world in every detail, and that you made us in your own image so that we could enjoy a very special relationship together. Please open our eyes, our minds and our hearts to the wonderful things you have made. In Jesus' name. Amen

In the beginning

Some people might think that God must have been terribly lonely and bored on his own, before he had created all the living things in the world. Perhaps they imagine him sitting in a chair, looking at the clock, wondering how to fill his time... picking up yet another crossword puzzle! Others might think, 'Bliss—a life of peace and quiet, no one to interrupt or interfere.' It's a bit like being shipwrecked on a desert island in the sun: some would like it, some would hate it. But there we go again, trying to contain God within our human limitations and understanding. God is God!

When we say that God has always existed, we mean that God the Father, Jesus the Son, and the Holy Spirit have always existed in unity together... and they all played a part in creation. Think about the discussion that might have taken place, at the time.

'Shall we make the earth flat?'

'We could make it round, square or triangular. That would be interesting—give the scientists something to argue about!'

'Shall we have creatures walking on the dry land, flying in the air or swimming in the water, or all three?'

Well, whatever happened, there wouldn't have been any disagreement.

Obviously, things had to be created in the correct order, otherwise there would have been all sorts of problems. Imagine...

'I've made the fish, but the water isn't finished yet. What am I going to do?'

The story of creation in Genesis shows God creating the world one thing at a time, in perfect order.

On the first day, he created the light so that life could begin. On the second day, he separated the water, to make sky and sea. On the third day, he created dry land, and all kinds of wonderful plants to grow on it. On the fourth day, he created the sun and the moon so that there could be day and night. On the fifth day, he created the sea creatures and all the birds that fly in the air. On the sixth day, he created the creatures that walk, run, hop... and every other form of movement... on the dry land.

Then God paused and said, 'There is one more thing that I have planned to create, and it's going to be very special. I'm going to make people, and the reason that they are going to be special is that I am going to make them like me in many ways, so that we can be close friends with each other.'

And so God made people in his own image, with personalities, the ability to think and love, the need to have a good relationship with him, and a conscience. What's a conscience? Well, it's like a little voice inside us that tells us when something we're about to do is wrong.

When the work of creation had been finished, God the Father, Jesus the Son, and the Holy Spirit looked at all their handiwork, and exclaimed, 'Hey! It's very good, isn't it? Especially the people—aren't they good?'

Then God felt that it was time to have a rest. It's good to keep one day a week special so that we can rest and spend time with God.

So God's work of creation was completed—perfectly, beautifully and in intricate detail—and he looked forward to sharing a wonderful friendship with the people that he had created.

Reproduced with permission from *Stories to Read Aloud* published by BRF 2004 (1 84101 362 5)

Taking care of God's creation

Teacher's information

 Bible reference

The story is based on Genesis 2:4–25.

 Theme

God instructs Adam to take care of the garden.

 Key verse

The Lord God put the man in the Garden of Eden to take care of it and to look after it.
GENESIS 2:15

 Talk about…

Ways in which we are damaging the world where we live.

 Aim

To value and take care of our environment.

> **Jigsaw puzzled**
>
> *Dear God…*
> *Does it matter if we spoil your creation?*

 Activitime

Beforehand, arrange for a volunteer to bring in a small pet and talk about taking care of it.

 Jigsaw piece

We read in the Bible that the first man and woman God created were Adam and Eve. God created Adam first, and made a wonderful garden for him to live in, called the garden of Eden. But Adam is lonely, so God decides to find him a companion.

> **Prayback**
>
> *Loving heavenly Father,*
> *Thank you for your wonderful creation, but please forgive us for not taking care of it as we should—through wasting valuable resources… by polluting the environment… by endangering wildlife for the sake of modern development… and for being greedy and not sharing with those who are in need. Help us to change our ways for the better. In Jesus' name. Amen*

You choose

'But I'm lonely, God! When you're not here, I've got no one to talk to,' Adam moaned, pulling a very long, sad face.

God thought for a while.

'I'll tell you what,' he replied, 'I've got a little job for you to do, and it may even solve the problem.'

Adam looked worried.

'What do you mean by a "little job"?' he enquired. 'I'm already quite busy doing the gardening.'

God smiled.

'Well, it's like this,' he said. 'I've made all these creatures in the garden, but I haven't named them yet. It needs doing! There's only a few *thousand*, some on the land, some in the air, and of course some in the water—it won't take too long.' God paused for a moment, deep in thought.

'You never know,' he continued, 'you might be able to find a creature to keep you company.'

Adam didn't know where to start. There were so many creatures, and all so different— long necks, short necks, spots, stripes, numerous colours, some that swam, some that walked, some that flew…

'What are you going to call this one?' God called, as he stood holding a large four-legged animal with big hairy hooves, quite a long neck, two large humps, and some horrible-looking green slime dribbling from its mouth.

Adam rubbed his chin, hoping for inspiration. You see, he'd got no experience of this kind of work.

'A slobberor… a humpy-backed… a hairy-legged… I know,' he said, at last. 'I'll call this one a *camel*.'

'A camel it is,' God replied. 'One down… lots to go!'

A few days later came the last one. God brought a small wiggly sea-creature with a hard skin and lots of legs. Adam was pleased that the job was coming to an end, so he decided to call it the first thing that came into his head.

'It's very small—I'll call it a *shrimp*!' he shouted out.

So the job was finished, much to Adam's relief. He felt like having a nice meal to celebrate—but not on his own.

'Any that you fancy as a companion?' God enquired.

'Well, they're all very nice. I love them all,' Adam sighed, 'but I really wanted something more like me to keep me company.'

So God made a woman—and she was called Eve.

Adam and Eve seemed very happy together in the garden of Eden. God had worked hard and made everything so beautifully.

'I'll see you both later,' God told them, as he was about to leave the garden. 'Be good, and remember to take care of things, particularly the creatures.'

'We will,' they both promised.

The deceiver

Teacher's information

 Bible reference

The story is based on Genesis 3:1–24.

 Theme

Adam and Eve disobey God as a result of the devil's deceit.

 Key verse

The Lord God then asked the woman, 'What have you done?' 'The snake tricked me,' she answered. 'And I ate some of that fruit.'
GENESIS 3:13

 Talk about...

Ways in which the devil deceives us to do foolish things through peer pressure—for example, stealing, taking drugs and so on.

 Aim

To look to God for what is true.

Jigsaw puzzled

Dear God...
Why are things often not what they appear to be?

 Activitime

Two volunteers are needed to perform a drama together in front of everyone. One has to pretend to be a salesperson trying to sell a totally useless product to a customer. He or she has to persuade the customer to buy it, by making the product appear to be what it isn't.

 Jigsaw piece

After creating the world, God made a garden called the garden of Eden for the first man and woman (Adam and Eve) to live in. This story is all about what happens in the garden—something that has a lasting and devastating effect on God's creation.

Prayback

God of truth,
We thank you that you have a wonderful plan for your creation, one that includes us. Please help us to realize that everything you say to us in the Bible is true, and all the things that you want us to do are to help that plan to be fulfilled.
Help us to recognize when the devil is deceiving us through the words of other people, trying to get us to do things that will be harmful to ourselves or those around us. Give us the strength to say 'NO!'
Thank you that you sent Jesus to repair the damage done by disobedience and evil. In Jesus' name. Amen

It's all lies

'What have you got planned for today, my darling?' Eve asked her husband, Adam, as they ate breakfast in the sunshine.

'I've got one or two small gardening jobs to be done, then I'll probably go for a swim,' he replied.

God had set out a beautiful garden for Adam and Eve to live in, full of wonderful plants and creatures. There was no fighting among the animals. There was no weeding to do, because all the plants were given their place. No one fell ill or died. The garden provided all the food and drink that was needed, and, best of all, God used to come and walk there every evening. There was only one rule to be obeyed—no one must eat from one particular tree that stood in the middle of the garden. Adam and Eve were responsible for looking after everything there in the garden of Eden.

As Adam went off to work, Eve decided to go out and pick some flowers for the house. Well, they called it a house—it was really just a clearing in the trees where they had their meals and slept. There were so many amazing flowers in fantastic colours, Eve really didn't know where to start. Then suddenly, she heard a voice.

'How can you choose from such a wonderful selection?' it said.

Eve turned round to see a rather beautiful snake nearby, but she didn't realize that it was the devil in disguise. He was in the garden to try to turn Adam and Eve against God, by using lies and deceit.

'God has been very good to us,' Eve replied, smiling contentedly.

'Tell me,' the snake continued, as he pointed with his tail to the variety of fruit-laden trees around the garden, 'is it true that God doesn't allow you to eat the fruit from any of these trees?'

The devil knew full well that that was not the case, but he was trying to sew a thread of doubt into Eve's mind.

'Oh no,' she answered. 'The only tree that we must not eat from is that one,' she continued, as she pointed to a large swaying tree, weighed down with the potential harvest. 'If we eat from that tree, it will spoil everything here.'

The snake was still for a moment, looking at the forbidden fruit and planning how he would deceive Eve.

'I can't see anything wrong with it myself,' he said, very persuasively. 'It looks as if it is ripe and juicy, and very good to eat, and I'm sure it won't spoil anything. Are you going to let God boss you about like this? Eat some and show him that you're as good as he is!'

'Well,' Eve replied, 'it is quite hot today and my throat does feel rather dry and rough, as if I've swallowed some sand.'

'Go on, then,' the snake hissed.

'You know what?' Eve responded defiantly. 'I will try some of the fruit. And what's more, I shall take some to Adam as well.'

Reproduced with permission from *Stories to Read Aloud* published by BRF 2004 (1 84101 362 5)

The devil slithered into a corner and laughed as he watched the two eat their way to their downfall. As soon as Adam and Eve had swallowed the fruit, the ecstasy that they had expected didn't happen. After all, what could be better than what they had already? Suddenly, they felt sick, deep down—not just a physical sickness, but a feeling of wishing that they could turn the clock back. They had disobeyed and let down the friend whom they loved so much—God. They felt guilty, dishonest, ashamed, frightened, and a million miles away from the God who loved them and had done so much for them. In that one act of dis-obedience, they had spoiled everything good that they had enjoyed in the past.

When God arrived later, Adam and Eve hid, because they were frightened, guilty and embarrassed about what had happened—and because they had suddenly realized that they were naked.

'Where are you?' God called out.

'Just getting dressed,' replied Adam. 'We'll be out in a minute.'

When Adam and Eve finally came out from behind some bushes, they had tried to tie a few large leaves together to wrap round themselves, in a very poor attempt to make clothes. If the situation hadn't been so sad, the sight of the two leaf-clad people would have been quite funny. They looked like overgrown cabbages.

God knew that things had changed, and why, but he still asked, 'What have you done, Adam? Have you disobeyed me and eaten the fruit I told you not to eat?'

'Not exactly,' Adam mumbled. 'What I mean is, yes, I did eat some of the fruit. But it has to be said that it was definitely the woman's fault for giving it to me.'

'Excuse me, yes, that is true to a point. But it was that snake over there that told me to eat it,' Eve added very quickly, pointing towards the accused.

'You're both responsible for your own actions,' God told them. 'Because you have disobeyed me, things have changed, sadly.'

From that time on, things like death, fear, shame, guilt, suffering, pain and separation from God affected his wonderful creation, because it had been damaged by disobedience.

'But I will put it all right one day,' God promised.

He had a plan to repair the brokenness through his Son, Jesus.

Reproduced with permission from *Stories to Read Aloud* published by BRF 2004 (1 84101 362 5)

Trusting in God's promises

 Bible reference

The story is based on Genesis 6:1—9:29.

 Theme

The rainbow is a sign that God will never flood the world again on such a large scale.

 Key verses

'When I send clouds over the earth, and a rainbow appears in the sky, I will remember my promise to you and to all other living creatures. Never again will I let flood waters destroy all life.' GENESIS 9:14–15

 Talk about…

Promises.

 Aim

To read about and trust in God's promises in the Bible.

Jigsaw puzzled

Dear God…
What does the rainbow mean?

 Activitime

Draw or paint a picture of your favourite animal, with a rainbow above it.

 Jigsaw piece

After Adam's and Eve's disobedience to God, it wasn't too many generations before people in the world turned their backs on him completely. They did some things that are very wrong. God decides that it is time to act.

Prayback

Faithful God,
Thank you that you have made so many wonderful promises to us and that the rainbow reminds us of one of them. Thank you that your promises never fail. Please help us to read about, believe and trust in those promises, and don't let the world ever become as bad as it was before the flood. In Jesus' name. Amen

Looks like rain!

'My poor little babies, are you thirsty? Mummy will get you a nice cool drink.'

'Is that you talking to the vegetables again?' Mr Noah called across the garden to his wife.

'Don't let me forget to water them later when the sun goes down!' Mrs Noah replied cheerfully, as she went to wash up the dishes from lunch.

As she was about to go in through the door, she turned round and added, 'And it's your turn to wash up at tea-time.'

Mr Noah was feeling full of fun, so, after he had waited a short while, he looked across to the kitchen window.

'Looks like rain,' he shouted to his wife, who was still inside the house tidying up. She came running out to where her husband stood.

'Where's the rain?' she asked enthusiastically. 'It's months since we've had any rain, and then it was just a shower.'

Mr Noah began to laugh and laugh and laugh, until the tears ran down his cheeks.

'Fooled you!' he said mischievously.

'Not funny! Not funny at all!' Mrs Noah chided as she returned to her housework—very cross.

The sound of pots and pans could be heard banging on to the draining board, perhaps a little louder than usual! The reason why Mrs Noah was so sensitive about rain was that, in the part of the world where Mr Noah and his family lived, there was very little rain, ever. There was nothing they would have liked more than a nice shower. Having said that, it came as quite a surprise to Mr Noah when God told him that he needed to build a big boat because there was going to be a flood.

God was very sad about the way that people had turned out. He had created them to do good things, to be kind and loving, to take care of his creation and to be friends with him. But all they seemed to want to do was turn their backs on him and behave in a selfish and greedy fashion.

'You and your family are the only ones who haven't turned their backs on me,' God told Mr Noah. 'Build an ark, then take your family and at least two of every kind of animal on board and stay there until the flood has gone

Reproduced with permission from *Stories to Read Aloud* published by BRF 2004 (1 84101 362 5)

down. Every other living thing will be drowned. Then we can make a fresh start.'

(In case you haven't already guessed, an ark is a kind of boat—it must have been a jolly big one!)

'Are you sure you heard him correctly?' Mrs Noah asked, when her husband began cutting trees down to make the boat. 'It's not likely that we will have that much rain—not here!'

'How many times must I repeat it to you?' Mr Noah replied, becoming a little agitated. 'God said, "Build a boat."'

'Whatever you say, dear,' came the reply.

Mrs Noah pulled one of her 'well, I suppose you know what you're doing' faces. However, before leaving her husband to it, she added, 'I'm surprised at God asking you to build an ark. He obviously hasn't seen the shed you built last year!'

The neighbours were even less kind about the boat builder, as they stood and jeered at him. 'Look at crazy old Noah,' they laughed, as they walked around holding out their hands, pretending to feel raindrops falling from the bright blue sky.

But Mr Noah trusted God—and if God said that there would be a flood, then a boat had to be built! Mr Noah was obedient, right down to the last detail—the type of wood, the dimensions, and the way it should be constructed. It looked a bit like an enormous barn set on top of an equally large fishing boat.

You might be thinking that poor old Mr Noah had quite a chase, catching all the animals that were to go aboard the ark, but it wasn't quite like that. God, who created all the animals, had control of the situation. When the time was right, all the creatures came of their own free will and went up into the ark to join Mr Noah and his family. When all the passengers were loaded, God shut the door… and the rain began to fall.

Suddenly, Mr Noah was very popular with his neighbours, but it was too late. Before long, their wooden houses floated by the ark in pieces, just like shipwrecks at sea.

It rained for forty days, so you can guess… the earth was well and truly flooded. However, God was faithful to Mr Noah, his family and all the animals in the ark. Though it took quite a while for the water to go down when the rain eventually stopped falling, God kept his promise to Mr Noah. He took care of the party aboard the big boat and even showed them when it was safe to come out.

'It's OK,' God said when they came out, 'I won't do that again.' And to remind us of his promise not to flood the whole earth again, God sent a rainbow.

Reproduced with permission from *Stories to Read Aloud* published by BRF 2004 (1 84101 362 5)

God is in control

Teacher's information

 ### Bible reference

The story is based on Genesis 11:1–9.

 ### Theme

God controls the power of the people, stopping the project because their motivation is selfish and with no moral restraint.

 ### Key verses

So the people had to stop building the city, because the Lord confused their language and scattered them all over the earth. That's how the city of Babel got its name.
GENESIS 11:8–9

 ### Talk about...

Ways in which scientific knowledge has been, and still is being, misused.

 ### Aim

Not to lose sight of God and his values.

Jigsaw puzzled

Dear God...
Is science getting out of control?

 ### Activitime

In groups, take it in turns to communicate a book or film title to the rest of the group without using spoken or written language. It's not very easy!

 ### Jigsaw piece

In the Bible, this story comes just after the story of Noah. In some ways, it is a similar story: people have become very self-centred and lost sight of the values of God. However, people have also become very powerful by working together—with greed as their motive. God feels that it is time to put a stop to it. (The tower in the story is known as the tower of Babel.)

Prayback

Almighty God,
Thank you for the story of the tower of Babel. Please let it be a warning to us not to ignore you or the rules that you have given to us for our benefit. Help us to do things for the right reasons and not out of selfish motives. And give the whole of our society an awareness that not all scientific developments are helpful. Thank you that you are still in control. In Jesus' name. Amen

No ordinary building

'Imagine going up all those stairs… with my back!'

'Isn't it high?'

'I wouldn't want to have to clean all those windows.'

Not that they'd have had glass in the windows in Bible times—but you know the sort of remarks that people make about really high buildings when they don't know what else to say!

This was no ordinary high building, either. It was so high that it went up into the clouds— part of a huge city that the people were building. In some ways, it was quite wonderful. Everyone was working together and they were making very good progress. However, there was a problem. The people seemed to have turned their backs on God. They weren't building the city and tower to help homeless people or provide hospital care for those who were unwell. No, it was all part of a plan to boost their own importance.

As God looked upon the situation, he saw the whole community becoming more and more powerful, but with no thought for his values. Power with no rules is what many people these days call 'freedom', but it is actually bound to lead to serious problems.

'The tower nearly reaches the sky now,' the builders shouted to each other in great excitement, feeling very proud of themselves. And I must say, they were doing pretty well.

It would seem that this was one of the few occasions when everyone in the community was in agreement. But God saw the danger of such power and decided to put a stop to it. He very cunningly introduced different languages into the massive building site—you can imagine the chaos! No one had a clue what was being said. It was a bit like watching a

foreign film with no subtitles.

Well, people could no longer understand each other, which soon put a stop to their building—much to God's relief. Needless to say, the project was never finished, but there are some important things to learn from this story. Power without a few simple rules is a very dangerous thing, as history has proved time and time again. Good communication is essential for any project to succeed—and God is still in control of the world today.

Reproduced with permission from *Stories to Read Aloud* published by BRF 2004 (1 84101 362 5)

Obedience to God

Teacher's information

 ### Bible reference

The story is based on Genesis 22:1–19.

 ### Theme

Abraham proves his obedience to God by showing that he is prepared to sacrifice his own son, Isaac, if it is God's will.

 ### Key verse

'Don't hurt the boy or harm him in any way!' the angel said. 'Now I know that you truly obey God, because you were willing to offer him your only son.'
GENESIS 22:12

 ### Talk about…

Things that we might find hard to give to God—for example, giving our holiday money to a missionary organization, or spending time in church instead of playing football.

 ### Aim

To obey God, despite the cost to us.

Jigsaw puzzled

Dear God…
Should I obey you even when it doesn't seem to make sense to me?

 ### Activitime

Five volunteers who like chocolate are needed! Hand a chocolate bar to each of the five, giving a good build-up but saying that they must not eat the chocolate yet. Then tell the five volunteers to go and give the chocolate bars away to people who weren't given any. As the faces fall and the five begin to move towards the others, call them back. Provide a second (substitute) chocolate bar for them to give away, so that they can each keep the first.

 ### Jigsaw piece

Having been told by God that his descendants would be a great nation, Abraham and his wife Sarah are overjoyed at the birth of their son, Isaac. So God's request, described in this story, comes as quite a surprise to Abraham.

Prayback

Faithful heavenly Father,
Thank you for sending your only Son, Jesus, to die on the cross in our place so that we might be forgiven for the wrong things that we have done.
Please help us to trust in your promises, even when we don't understand why things are happening to us that may not be very nice. Make us obedient to your will. In Jesus' name. Amen

A test from God

'Who'd have believed it?' Abraham repeated excitedly, as he sat in his rocking chair drinking his cocoa—or whatever they drank in those days.

'Who'd have believed what?' his wife Sarah asked, a little impatiently.

'I was just thinking about us, both in our 90s and expecting our first baby,' he replied, as he pretended to cradle a small child in his arms.

'We'll be the oldest parents waiting at the school gate, anyway!' the mother-to-be mused. Then she smiled. 'It is rather exciting!' she agreed.

With that, they began to dream away the evening. Sarah thought about making pretty clothes for the infant, going for long walks in the sunshine, and watching the child grow up. Abraham remembered God's promise to him, that through him a nation of people would arise who would follow God.

Time passed by, until it was the moment that most fathers look forward to with fear and trepidation. It was in the middle of the night when Sarah prodded Abraham in the ribs with her elbow to wake him up.

'I think it's time, my dear,' she told him firmly.

Abraham was just about to ask, 'Time for what?' when he suddenly realized that she meant the baby was about to be born. Abraham began flapping around, muttering, 'Towels and hot water, towels and hot water.'

'Just go and get the midwife,' Sarah instructed him, taking control of things.

One sock on, one sock off, dressing-gown blowing in the wind, Abraham went hopping up the road, doing as he was told. Anyway, all was well. Sarah had a baby boy and they called him Isaac.

As Isaac grew up, Abraham did all the kinds of things that fathers do with their sons: played games with him, told him stories, taught him things, came last in races... what they call father–son bonding today! Abraham thought the world of his son and so it came as quite a shock when God told him about an important task that he had for Abraham to do.

'We're going into the mountains,' Abraham told Isaac the next day. 'God wants us to make a burnt offering to him.' Isaac knew what a burnt offering was: an animal would be killed and burnt on an altar, as an offering to God. Then God would forgive the family for the wrong things that they had done.

There was one thing that Isaac didn't understand, though—his father hadn't got a lamb ready to take with them. What Isaac didn't know was that *he* was to be the sacrifice. That's what God had instructed Abraham to do. How could Abraham father a great nation if he sacrificed his and Sarah's only son? What would he say to his wife? What a test of faith and obedience for Abraham!

The father and son walked to the spot where the sacrifice and burnt offering were to be performed.

'Let's build the altar here,' Abraham said to

Reproduced with permission from *Stories to Read Aloud* published by BRF 2004 (1 84101 362 5)

Isaac sadly. 'You go and get some wood for the fire.'

Feeling very important, Isaac ran off to find some twigs and broken branches. Abraham could hardly contain his deep sorrow, but he was sure that God had a good reason for telling him to make an offering of his son. When everything was prepared, Abraham tied Isaac up and laid him on the wood, ready to perform the deed.

'What are you doing, Dad?' the young lad asked, thinking that Abraham was having a joke. 'I feel like a chicken, about to be cooked for dinner.'

But then Abraham raised the knife, ready to plunge into Isaac, and the lad realized it wasn't a joke. Isaac's cries of fear were interrupted as an angel cried out, 'Abraham, Abraham. Don't harm the boy. You have demonstrated your faith and obedience to God by being prepared to do this. There is a ram over there that you can use instead.'

Abraham was so relieved. After sacrificing the ram and making a burnt offering of it, Abraham turned to Isaac.

'Let's go home, son,' he said. 'Your mother will be wondering where we are.'

'Bet you're glad you haven't got to explain to Mum that you'd sacrificed me to God,' the lad laughed, still a little shaken by the experience.

And so they returned home, ready for God to work out his plan for Abraham because of his faith and obedience.

'Guess what?' Sarah said when they walked up the path. 'Chicken for tea!'

Reproduced with permission from *Stories to Read Aloud* published by BRF 2004 (1 84101 362 5)

7

Family relationships

Teacher's information

 Bible reference

The story is based on Genesis 25:27–34 and Genesis 27:1–45.

 Theme

Jacob's deceit has a very damaging effect on the relationships within the family.

 Key verse

Esau hated his brother Jacob because he had stolen the blessing that was supposed to be his. So he said to himself, 'Just as soon as my father dies, I'll kill Jacob.'
GENESIS 27:41

 Talk about…

Things that cause arguments in families.

 Aim

To work hard at the relationships in our families.

> **Jigsaw puzzled**
>
> *Dear God…*
> *Why can't I behave just as I like at home?*

 Activitime

Draw a family tree, including as many of your family as you can.

 Jigsaw piece

Several years after nearly being sacrificed to God by his father, Isaac got married and had two sons—Jacob and Esau. This is the story about a family divided by lies and deceit, all caused by greed.

> **Prayback**
>
> *God of love,*
> *We thank you that it was your idea that we should be part of a family, and that within that unit we should find love, security, discipline and many other necessary things. We thank you for the other members of our families, even though they are no more perfect than we are.*
> *Please help us to be generous, kind, co-operative and honest with our relatives and always to try to build up those relationships, even when it seems difficult. Be with families who have split up, or are going through difficult times at the moment. In Jesus' name. Amen*

Stew and dumplings

Isaac was sitting in his favourite armchair one day. He was very old. His hair and beard were as white as snow. Everything seemed to be wearing out. His joints were so stiff, they creaked like old farm gates. He couldn't hear well, so everyone had to shout when they spoke to him. He found it more difficult to get his breath than he used to, so he ended up puffing as soon as he exerted himself in any way, and he was nearly blind.

One day, Isaac realized that there were things he had to sort out before he died, so he called the elder of his two grown-up sons.

'Esau!'

After a moment, a distant reply came. 'Yes, father?'

The old man missed the reply. Once again, he called. 'Esau, where are you, my son?'

Esau rushed into the room and went over to where Isaac was sitting. He placed his hand on his father's arm.

'Here I am,' he assured Isaac.

The old man sighed a sigh of relief.

'I'm getting on in years now,' Isaac told his son. 'I do not have much longer to live.'

'You've got years left in you yet,' Esau laughed, trying to cheer up his old dad.

'Don't interrupt me, boy!' Isaac scolded his son, treating him as if he were a small child again. 'I'm a little peckish. Go out hunting and then make me a nice stew and dumplings. After that, I need to talk to you about your "blessing".'

As the elder son, it was Esau's right to be given all the family money and possessions when his father died, and to receive a special blessing. Esau knew what was to come: his father was going to ask God to give him that blessing as the new head of the family. Excitedly, Esau hurried out with his bow and arrow—no time to waste! Perhaps I should add that Esau didn't want his father to die, but he did want the blessing.

While all this had been going on, someone's ear had been pressed up against the door, listening. Rebekah, Esau's and Jacob's mum, had heard every single word.

Jacob was a bit of a mummy's boy, so Rebekah ran to find him immediately, to tell him what was happening. She knew that Jacob had already tricked Esau into giving him the family fortune. One day, when Esau had come home really hungry, he had foolishly agreed to let Jacob have his inheritance in return for a meal. Now all Jacob needed to go with it was the blessing.

'There's no time to lose,' Rebekah told Jacob. 'Do as I tell you, quickly.'

She instructed her younger son to bring in two goats from the flock.

'I will prepare a nice stew and dumplings,' Rebekah told Jacob. 'Then you can take it to your father before Esau does. When you have done that, your father will give the blessing to you, rather than to your brother.'

'Father may be short-sighted,' answered

Reproduced with permission from *Stories to Read Aloud* published by BRF 2004 (1 84101 362 5)

Jacob, 'but he's not stupid. My brother's body is hairy, like a woolly bear's. If father touches my arms or neck, he'll soon know that I'm not Esau—my arms are smooth and soft! Besides which, Esau *smells* like a bear!'

'Just do as you're told. I know what I'm doing,' Rebekah commanded.

Jacob felt quietly confident, knowing that his mother had a plan. But it has to be said that the two goats weren't going to be very happy about their involvement.

When Jacob brought in the goats, Rebekah prepared the meal for her husband, Isaac.

'Put these on,' she said, thrusting a pile of Esau's clothes into Jacob's arms. 'Oh, and I've made you some goatskin gloves and a scarf. They will make your hands and neck feel hairy!'

Tray in hand, dressed in Esau's clothes and the pieces of goatskin, Jacob went into the room where his father was sitting. He looked ridiculous and smelt even worse!

'Dinner's ready,' he called nervously.

'Is that you, Jacob?' his father asked.

'No, it's me, Esau,' Jacob said defiantly.

Isaac was not convinced. The voice sounded just like Jacob's.

'You're pulling my leg,' Isaac laughed. 'It is Jacob, isn't it?'

There was a moment's silence. Jacob didn't know what to do next.

'Come here, let me touch your arm, boy,' Isaac asked, holding his hands out to Jacob.

Isaac felt the hairy goatskin on his son's arms.

'Are you really Esau?' Isaac asked once again.

'Of course I am,' Jacob replied. 'Would I lie to my own father?'

Isaac ate his dinner. It was very tasty.

'Before I fall asleep, come over and kiss me, my son,' Isaac requested.

As Jacob kissed his father, Isaac smelt the aroma of Esau's clothes and the goatskin.

'Ah yes!' Isaac sighed contentedly. 'That's my Esau. Always smells like a dead camel!'

With that, Isaac gave Jacob the blessing to go with his inheritance and put him in charge of the whole family.

Jacob had been so selfish. He had lied to his father and he had cheated his brother out of something that was rightfully his. It was sure to split the family up when Esau found out what had happened.

Then came a knock at the door. It was Jacob's brother, Esau, with a plate of stew and dumplings for his father...

'DINNER IS SERVED!'

Reproduced with permission from *Stories to Read Aloud* published by BRF 2004 (1 84101 362 5)

8

The destructiveness of jealousy

Teacher's information

 ### Bible reference

The story is based on Genesis 37:1–36.

 ### Theme

Joseph's brothers hate him because their father loves Joseph more than he loves them.

 ### Key verses

Jacob loved Joseph more than he did any of his other sons, because Joseph was born after Jacob was very old. Jacob had given Joseph a fine coat to show that he was his favourite son, and so Joseph's brothers hated him and would not be friendly to him.
GENESIS 37:3–4

 ### Talk about…

The kind of things that make people jealous.

 ### Aim

Not to be jealous or do things that make others jealous.

Jigsaw puzzled

Dear God…
Is there anything wrong with wanting what someone else has got?

 ### Activitime

Provide the following visual aids as a lead-in to the story.

- A dish of brightly coloured sweets to hand round
- A model of a sheaf of corn, made with either real corn or drinking straws
- A picture of the sun, moon and eleven stars

Explain that in the story a brightly coloured gift is given, and that there is an incident involving a sheaf of corn and another involving the sun, moon and eleven stars.

 ### Jigsaw piece

After cheating his brother out of his inheritance, Jacob eventually married and had many children, but his favourite child was Joseph. This story is all about the continuing family problems in Joseph's generation, caused by favouritism.

Prayback

God who loves us all,
Thank you for the story about Joseph. Please help us not to be jealous of others or to make others jealous of us. Enable us to build up the relationships that we have with the other members of our families and with you, our Father in heaven. In Jesus' name. Amen

Nice coat!

'Joseph, Joseph, can you come in here for a moment,' Jacob called to his son.

Joseph was just getting ready to help his brothers take the sheep out to graze on the hillside.

'Oh no!' the brothers all said in unison, except for one—he just sighed an enormous sigh.

They had already been waiting for half an hour for Joseph to emerge from the house, and he'd only just that minute wandered out, as if 'next week would do'. The boy had probably only scrambled out of bed a few minutes previously, and now their father was calling him back in.

'You'll have to wait a bit longer for me now,' Joseph shouted, laughing as he went inside again.

The brothers were furious and sat themselves down on the dusty ground—yet again! Even the sheep seemed to 'baa' in frustration.

It must be said that Joseph's brothers had a tough time of it. Joseph was Jacob's favourite son. I know that there shouldn't be favouritism, but that's the way it was. The lad was 17 and he had the best of everything, which certainly caused quite a lot of jealousy in the family. He was never expected to work as hard as the others, and he always stayed in bed longer than them in the mornings. Maybe that's why he seemed to have so many dreams! Unfortunately for his brothers, they weren't the kind of dreams that are forgotten by the morning.

Anyway, suddenly the front door opened.

'Ahh! My eyes!' one of the brothers shouted, as he pretended to shield his face with his forearm.

'Must be raining,' another yelled, as he pointed at Joseph. 'There's a rainbow over there!'

All the brothers creased up laughing as Joseph marched out of the front door wearing the brightest, most colourful coat you could ever imagine.

'Dad's bought me a new coat,' he announced.

'So we see,' replied one of the brothers, covering up his true feelings of intense jealousy at the way the young lad was spoiled by Jacob. 'You won't get run over by a camel in that.'

'Apart from wanting to give me a migraine with your bright coat, why are you so late this morning?' one of the brothers asked Joseph, as they walked the sheep to the hillside.

'Well, it's funny you should ask,' Joseph replied.

'Oh, it's funny you should ask,' mimicked one of the others.

However, the brothers soon realized that it had probably been a mistake to ask the question.

'I had a dream last night,' Joseph said in an arrogant manner. 'I dreamed that we were

Reproduced with permission from *Stories to Read Aloud* published by BRF 2004 (1 84101 362 5)

helping in the harvest field and your sheaves of corn bowed down to mine.'

'You needn't think that we'd ever bow down to you,' one of the brothers growled, with hatred in his voice.

There was a strange sort of atmosphere after that—the kind that you get after a big row.

The next day was even tenser, because Joseph had had a similar dream, involving the sun, moon and eleven stars. As it happened, God was going to use Joseph in a wonderful way to save his family from a famine, but that didn't help the immediate situation.

Jacob continued to spoil Joseph, Joseph continued to be rather arrogant, and his brothers' jealousy and hatred just grew and grew and grew… until eventually they played a terrible trick to get rid of him. First of all, they pulled off his fine coat and threw him into a dry well, and then they sold him as a slave to a passing group of slave traders who were on their way to Egypt.

'Well, that's an end to "rainbow boy" and his stupid dreams,' one of the brothers commented.

'Let's tell Dad that Joseph has been killed by a wild animal,' another suggested. So that's what they did. And that's where jealousy can lead!

Reproduced with permission from *Stories to Read Aloud* published by BRF 2004 (1 84101 362 5)

9

Making a difference in the world

 Bible reference

The story is based on Genesis 39:1–23.

 Theme

Joseph is obedient to God and does his best in everything, which makes a big impression on his Egyptian master.

 Key verses

So Joseph lived in the home of Potiphar, his Egyptian owner. Soon Potiphar realized that the Lord was helping Joseph to be successful in whatever he did.
GENESIS 39:2–3

 Talk about…

Things we can do to help others.

 Aim

To do our best in everything to help other people.

Jigsaw puzzled

Dear God…
Does it make a difference when I do my best?

 Activitime

Draw a picture of a house. Inside the house, list all the ways in which you could be more helpful in the home—for example, by washing up, tidying your room and so on.

 Jigsaw piece

After Joseph's brothers have sold him to slave traders, he is taken to Egypt to be sold on as a slave.

Prayback

Living God,
*   Thank you for Joseph's example to us. Sometimes we find ourselves having to do things that we don't want to do. But please help us still to do our best to do things your way and with a willingness to help others. Help us to make the world a better place, as we, and other people, follow Joseph's example. In Jesus' name. Amen*

Do your best

Joseph is the young lad whose father bought him a very brightly coloured coat to wear. Maybe today you wouldn't think that a coat like that was particularly trendy, but in those days it was just what Joseph needed to tell everyone that he was his father's favourite son. Joseph did boast rather a lot to his older brothers and, as a result, he was not very popular with them. His dreams were the last straw, but that's another story.

We join the story after Joseph had been sold as a slave to a group of traders, and ended up in Egypt.

'I want someone who is smart, reliable and strong, please,' a very important-looking gentleman asked the slave dealers. 'I am captain of the palace guard. I need a slave that can be trusted.'

'All our slaves are good, sir,' a rather nervous trader answered.

'I don't want any ruffians,' continued the gentleman, whose name was Potiphar.

'Perhaps sir would like to take this young man,' the trader replied, pushing Joseph towards him. 'Look at his hands—not a blemish. He's educated.'

Potiphar pondered for a while. He had been caught out before with slaves—a bit like buying a second-hand car today!

'Can I exchange him for another if he's no good?' Potiphar enquired.

'If you can find us, we'll exchange him,' the trader replied, grinning rather mischievously.

'What price are you asking for him?' Potiphar demanded.

The merchant whispered a figure in his ear.

'How much?' Potiphar shouted. 'I could get one just like him for half the price down the road. In fact, the traders there are doing a special offer—buy two, get one free!'

But a few whispers later a price was agreed.

'Come with me, boy,' the captain of the palace guard instructed, as he led the young man back to his house.

Now Joseph could have been difficult. He'd been spoiled by his dad, kidnapped by his brothers, bought by traders, taken to a foreign land and sold as a slave. He could have taken the attitude, 'Why should I?' But he didn't. Joseph had been brought up to trust God and to know his ways, so he was determined that he was going to live according to the standards of God in his new home and do his best in everything.

'I may not have chosen to be here, away from my family,' Joseph said to himself, 'but I'm going to be the best slave ever.'

And Joseph was such a good slave that Potiphar put him in charge of his whole household. He was like a housekeeper and farm manager all rolled into one!

'We are all slaves, but we can still take a pride in our work,' Joseph would tell the other servants. 'Let's make sure that the house is cleaner than ever before, that the food is prepared and presented with excellence, that the livestock are cared for without cutting corners, and that in everything we do we are honest.'

A few of the servants gasped in horror. One of them just said, 'Oh!' in a very loud voice.

If there were any arguments about jobs to be done, Joseph would say, 'Do I ever ask you to do anything that I would not do myself?'

All the other slaves had to agree that he never did. Not only did everything run smoothly with Joseph in charge, but he carried out his daily duties so cheerfully, willingly and thoroughly that the whole household seemed to be a better place because of it.

Sadly, however, Potiphar's wife didn't always tell the truth. One day, she told lies about Joseph to get him into trouble because he wouldn't do as she wanted. Everyone believed her word against his, so Joseph was put into prison… and he transformed the prison into a better place, in the same way that he had transformed Potiphar's household.

Joseph was able to make a difference in Potiphar's household and in the prison because he trusted God. He lived according to God's values and he did his best. Perhaps we can 'make a difference' as well, if we follow Joseph's example.

Reproduced with permission from *Stories to Read Aloud* published by BRF 2004 (1 84101 362 5)

10

The right person in the right place at the right time

Teacher's information

 ### Bible reference

The story is based on Exodus 1:1—2:10.

 ### Theme

God places Moses in the care of the king's daughter, to grow up in the royal household.

 ### Key verse

And when he was old enough, she took him to the king's daughter, who adopted him. She named him Moses because she said, 'I pulled him out of the water.'
EXODUS 2:10

 ### Talk about…

Times when we've been in the 'right place' at the 'right time'.

 ### Aim

Not always to put things down to coincidence.

Jigsaw puzzled

Dear God…
Is it just luck when I seem to be in the right place at the right time?

 ### Activitime

Bring a small shrub or tree in a pot, having arranged for the group to plant it somewhere nearby. Plan the exact location carefully together, because it will be a long-term investment. Where will your tree look nice in five or ten years' time, when it's grown much bigger?

 ### Jigsaw piece

After being put into prison, Joseph was eventually released and put into a position of authority in Egypt. As a result of that, his people, the Israelites, moved to Egypt to escape a famine. The Israelites become very prosperous, until a new king comes into power many years later.

Prayback

Compassionate God,
We thank you that sometimes you put us into a position where we can help someone. Please encourage us to make good use of those opportunities. In Jesus' name. Amen

Problems

After Joseph died, the Israelites experienced many years of prosperity in Egypt and slowly increased in number. But then... a new king came to power in Egypt.

The new king called a meeting of his government and said, 'Have you noticed that we are getting outnumbered by these Israelites? They are becoming a threat. Maybe if we put slave masters over them and worked them hard, they might not be so healthy. What do you think?'

Heads nodded in quiet agreement.

'We will put them into slavery. They will work in the fields, make bricks, build houses... and we can put our feet up,' the new king continued, with a chuckle.

His colleagues rubbed their hands together, grinning from ear to ear, like cats that had got the cream.

Months later, the king met with his government once again. 'How is it all going?' he asked. 'Are the Israelites dying off now?'

'Umm! Not exactly,' came the nervous reply.

'What?' the king roared, banging his fist down on to the table with a noise that sounded like thunder.

The table wobbled and fell over, with only three of the four legs still intact.

'The more we make them suffer, the healthier they seem to be,' one of the officials added, trembling slightly. 'I don't understand it!'

The king grabbed the official so tightly by the shoulder that the man's arm began to go numb. Just as the poor man began to whimper a little, the king let go, a smile creeping over his face.

'I have it!' the king shouted, making everyone jump. 'I will instruct the Egyptian midwives to kill all the Israelite baby boys as soon as they are born.'

There was some more rubbing of hands and grinning with sheer relief. The members of the government scurried out like rats to put the new scheme into operation.

'Oh, isn't he lovely?' smiled Shiphrah, the midwife, as she handed the newborn child to his mother. 'A lovely bouncing baby boy. Take good care of him.'

She hadn't got the heart to kill any of the Israelite children, and neither had any of the other midwives. Needless to say, the king's little plan was not successful. Back to the drawing board!

Another meeting of the government was called.

'I've been thinking,' the king began thoughtfully. 'If we were to tell all the Egyptian people to throw any Israelite boy babies that they see into the River Nile, perhaps that would cut down the number of Israelites in Egypt.'

There were a few doubts, but everyone was too scared to contradict the king, so the new law was passed.

Reproduced with permission from *Stories to Read Aloud* published by BRF 2004 (1 84101 362 5)

Of course, the Israelites all tried to hide their little boys to keep them alive. It was quite easy when they were very young, but it got more and more difficult as they grew older. One mother managed to hide her son until he was three months old, at which point he began to develop a rather powerful set of lungs. On a 'good' day, his cry was so loud that it caused the ornaments on the mantelpiece to vibrate.

'He won't stop crying,' his mother would say frantically, scared that one of the Egyptians would hear. One day, in desperation, she asked her family, 'What are we going to do?'

They thought deeply.

'I have an idea,' the baby's older sister said. 'There is a beautiful Egyptian princess who bathes in the River Nile each day, near the bulrushes. Maybe, if she saw him, she would feel sorry for him and look after him in the safety of the king's palace.'

'Don't be silly, darling,' her mother scolded. 'You're letting your imagination run away with you.'

'Has anyone got any better ideas?' the baby's father intervened.

It was so quiet, you could have heard a pin drop.

'That's decided, then,' he continued.

A little basket was made, suitably water-proofed and lined with comfortable bedding, and the baby was wrapped up warm inside. He was taken in the basket and placed in the bulrushes next to the River Nile. His sister watched from a distance.

Sure enough, the princess went down to bathe... *and the baby cried*! So the princess sent her slave girl to investigate. Well, when the baby was brought back, the princess only had to take one look.

'Oh, isn't he cute?' she exclaimed, already taking him up into her arms. 'Poor little thing. I must look after him.'

The baby's sister quickly rushed out to the princess, realizing that it was her only opportunity.

'Would you like me to find a nanny to look after the child for you?' she enquired.

'Sounds good to me!' replied the princess.

So guess who the sister went to get? Yes, the baby's mother! She was told to take the baby home until he was a bit older, and then the princess would bring him up as her son.

The princess called the baby Moses. He grew up in the king's palace, which was to be useful later on for a very special job that God had planned for him—but that's another story. Funny how God manages to get the right person into the right place at the right time, isn't it? Well, no, it's not really. That's God for you—quite amazing!

Reproduced with permission from *Stories to Read Aloud* published by BRF 2004 (1 84101 362 5)

11

Learning from our mistakes

Teacher's information

 Bible reference

The story is based on Exodus 3:1—4:31.

 Theme

Moses has spent several years away from Egypt, during which time God has been preparing him for a special mission. Moses has learned from things he has done wrong in the past. Now God feels that he is ready to perform that special task—and it's a huge one!

 Key verse

'Now go to the king! I am sending you to lead my people out of his country.'
EXODUS 3:10

 Talk about…

How we can learn from our mistakes.

 Aim

To put into practice the knowledge that we gain from times when we 'get it wrong'.

Jigsaw puzzled

Dear God…
Can you still use me, even though I make mistakes?

 Activitime

Bring in a tree branch and a bag of ashes, and point out the obvious: if the branch is set on fire, ashes will be left—because that is what happens!

 Jigsaw piece

For many years, the Israelites were slaves in Egypt. In the last story, Moses, who was an Israelite, was saved from death and put into a privileged position in the Egyptian palace. While he was growing up, he did some silly things and eventually ran away from Egypt. This story takes place in Midian some years later.

Prayback

God of forgiveness,
Thank you that we can always learn something positive from our mistakes. Please forgive us for the times when we have failed to behave in the way that you would like us to. Enable us to benefit from the knowledge that we have gained from those times, and help us do better in the future. In Jesus' name. Amen

Just another day

'Just another boring day, sitting on a rock in the desert, looking after the sheep,' thought Moses.

Of course, it was a bit of a comedown from having grown up in the palace. Moses felt so fed up—he had played all the games, counted sheep until he'd nearly fallen asleep, gone for little walks…

'I know,' he laughed. 'I'll see what my wife, Zipporah, has put in my sandwiches.'

He got out his lunch box in order to investigate. It was obvious what he'd got as soon as he opened the lid.

'Camel sandwiches again!' he sighed, as he picked up a rather strange-shaped snack. There were two large lumps sticking out at the top of it!

'I hate camel sandwiches,' he moaned. 'The camels are always so old and tough.'

Anyway, as he looked further, he smiled. 'Yum yum! Locusts with barbecue sauce,' he said out loud.

He paused. 'Listen to me, talking to a herd of noisy, smelly, moth-eaten sheep,' he continued.

Well, Moses felt a little peckish, so he took a large bite out of one of the sandwiches. As usual, they lived up to their name—the sand seemed to get everywhere! Can you imagine it—crunchy camel sandwiches?

Anyway, suddenly something caught Moses' eye.

'A bonfire!' he yelled, as he jumped up in excitement. It was just as if Christmas had come!

But there's nothing special about a bush that is on fire—or is there? Just as Moses began to sit down again, he realized that there was something very unusual about this one.

It wasn't just a question of 'who lit it in the middle of the desert?' No matter how long the bush burned, it remained intact. It looked a bit like the coal-effect gas fires that we have today. But apart from the fact that they hadn't been invented then, and there was no gas in the middle of the desert, either… it was just an ordinary bush. This was creepy—even miraculous!

Moses stood up, determined to investigate. His walk became a run…

Reproduced with permission from *Stories to Read Aloud* published by BRF 2004 (1 84101 362 5)

'Why doesn't this bush burn up into a pile of ash?' Moses thought as he approached it.

Then something even stranger happened. *A voice came from the bush.*

'That's far enough,' the voice said.

Well, Moses was about to turn round and run like a rabbit when the voice continued.

'Take your shoes off. You are in the presence of God.'

Poor old Moses was quite overwhelmed. It wasn't just another boring day, after all. Anyway, he thought he'd better take off his shoes, so, after some hopping and falling over a few times, Moses was ready to listen to God.

God and Moses had a lot of talking to do. It turned out that it had not gone unnoticed by God that the Israelites were suffering terrible things as slaves in Egypt. God wanted Moses to free the Israelites from the Egyptians and take them to the 'promised land'. The reason that things had taken so long would seem to be that Moses had taken rather a lot of time getting himself ready for the job—an awful lot of time! Mind you, it was to be a huge job!

Well, Moses did a bit of arguing (only to be expected). God did a few miracles and eventually Moses got to work. He'd changed a lot over the years—learned from his mistakes and failings. It's amazing how God uses even our mistakes and failings for good, and then he is able to use us to help fulfil his perfect plan for creation.

Reproduced with permission from *Stories to Read Aloud* published by BRF 2004 (1 84101 362 5)

12

Lack of faith

Teacher's information

 Bible reference

The story is based on Numbers 20:1–13.

 Theme

Moses and Aaron are forbidden to lead the Israelites into the promised land because of their lack of faith.

 Key verse

But the Lord said to Moses and Aaron, 'Because you refused to believe in my power, these people did not respect me. And so, you will not be the ones to lead them into the land I have promised.'
NUMBERS 20:12

 Talk about…

Times when we have been angry and done things that we have later regretted.

 Aim

Not to doubt the promises of God.

Jigsaw puzzled

Dear God…
What happens when we try to do things our way instead of yours?

 Activitime

Give everyone a drink and a biscuit.

 Jigsaw piece

After Moses has led the Israelites out of slavery in Egypt into the desert, the Israelites begin to do a lot of moaning about God to Moses.

Prayback

God of wisdom,
Thank you that your promises never fail. Please help us not to doubt them and not to end up doing things our way because we don't believe that your ways will work. In Jesus' name. Amen

Anyone for a drink?

It certainly is a terrible thing to be thirsty, although mostly we don't really know what it is like to be that desperate for something to drink. For the Israelites, out in the wilderness with Moses, the fear of dehydration was very much a reality. The sun was very hot and there was little or no shade. Everywhere was dry and sandy and water supplies were few and far between.

Well, on this particular day, the Israelites were having a good moan to poor old Moses and his brother, Aaron.

'I wish I'd died in Egypt,' one of the people said, as he looked around for some sympathy.

'Yes, why bring us and our animals out to the desert to die?' another asked.

'There's not many crops to be picked here and we're thirsty,' the angry mob complained.

'We loved making bricks in Egypt,' a middle-aged man shouted out. 'I know they called it slavery, but it wasn't real slavery—it's good to learn a trade.'

'Look at the muscles on my arms,' a rather large lady yelled, as she held up her arms to demonstrate. 'That's thanks to carrying lots and lots of bricks.'

Then everything went silent as a little boy walked up to Moses.

'How much longer do we have to travel across the desert?' the little boy pleaded.

It was true that when the Israelites had been set free from slavery in Egypt and begun their journey to the promised land, they hadn't expected to spend the next 40 years in the desert. However, in all fairness to God, he had been looking after them and they had never gone short, but these 'little grumbles' were not uncommon.

Moses' brother, Aaron, was about to slink off when he thought no one was looking, but Moses grabbed him by the arm.

'And where do you think you're going?' he asked. 'We'll go and pray about it,' he continued firmly, as he led Aaron away to a place where they could speak to God in peace.

'It's been another hard day,' Moses explained to God. 'The people are grumbling again. They say that they are thirsty.'

Reproduced with permission from *Stories to Read Aloud* published by BRF 2004 (1 84101 362 5)

Moses pretended to pull his hair out in frustration.

'You don't have to tell me,' God answered. 'I understand. What's new? They always moan, and I heard every word that they said.'

You see, God is everywhere, and he knows everything.

'Find your old staff again,' God commanded. 'The one that you have used before to perform miracles. Take the staff in your hand, gather everyone in front of the great rock and speak to it nicely—and water will pour out of the rock.'

So Moses, staff in hand, summoned everyone to the place that God had said. I have to say at this point that Moses' patience was wearing a bit thin. He was getting a bit touchy.

'Quiet, you rebellious lot!' Moses yelled.

Suddenly everyone in the crowd had that innocent look about them, as if to say, 'It wasn't me complaining!'

'Once again, I'm having to bow down to your whinging,' Moses shouted. 'As always!'

With that, he struck the rock violently with the staff, in anger and frustration.

Sure enough, the water came pouring out—it was almost like the Niagara Falls—and everyone drank. But God was not very pleased.

'Hey, Moses!' he said. 'And you, Aaron! I want a word with you both.'

Moses and Aaron were in trouble.

'I thought I told you to hold the staff in your hand, Moses, and speak to the rock,' God reprimanded. 'I didn't ask you to attack the rock.'

God was more disappointed than angry. He was sad that Moses hadn't trusted him enough just to do what he was told to do, knowing that God himself would do the rest. Also, God felt that Moses had shown disrespect for him by the way that he had abused the staff, which was very special.

With great regret, God told Moses and Aaron that, because of what they had done, they would not lead the Israelites into the promised land.

Reproduced with permission from *Stories to Read Aloud* published by BRF 2004 (1 84101 362 5)

13

The nature of love

Teacher's information

 Bible reference

The story is based on Ruth 1:1–22.

 Theme

Ruth demonstrates her love to Naomi, in the selfless commitment that she makes to her.

 Key verses

Ruth answered, 'Please don't tell me to leave you and return home! I will go where you go, I will live where you live; your people will be my people, your God will be my God. I will die where you die and be buried beside you. May the Lord punish me if we are ever separated, even by death!'
RUTH 1:16–17

 Talk about…

Situations when our love for other people could be put under strain.

 Aim

To be committed in our relationships.

Jigsaw puzzled

Dear God…
Can you make our relationships better?

 Activitime

Work out a 'group promise', for example, 'We promise to be helpful, kind and friendly.' Write it up on a large sheet of paper or card to hang on the wall. Don't break the promise!

 Jigsaw piece

Some of the greatest love stories ever told appear in the Bible. One of them, written in the Old Testament, is a very important story, because it involves the earthly ancestry of Jesus. It is the story of a young woman called Ruth. The significance of this part of the story of Ruth is to illustrate true love and commitment.

Prayback

Loving God,
We thank you that your love for us is wonderful. Please help us to love each other. Enable us to be committed to all the relationships that we have—our friends, our family, our neighbours… And heal those relationships that seem to have got broken or damaged. Fill us and the world with love for you and one another. In Jesus' name. Amen

A story of true love (Part One)

Long, long ago, more than a thousand years before the birth of Jesus, there was a terrible famine in the land of Israel. It hadn't rained for such a long time that most of the crops had failed. The countryside was no longer green and beautiful—everything had turned brown. Underfoot, the long grass was crunchy. It sounded as if you were walking on eggshells.

There was hardly anything for people to eat—and that included Elimelech and his family, who lived in Bethlehem.

'What's for tea, dear?' Elimelech asked his wife, Naomi, one day.

'The same as yesterday,' she replied, with a sigh. 'A piece of stale bread and some soup made from fish heads.'

'Oh no! Not again!' Mahlon and Chilion said in unison.

Mahlon and Chilion were Elimelech's and Naomi's two sons—growing lads!

'We can't stay here and starve to death,'

Naomi said quietly, with a tear in her eye. 'We must do something!'

Her husband sighed an enormous sigh. He felt as if he had let the whole family down, but it wasn't his fault.

'All right,' Elimelech replied. 'Tonight we will pack our bags, and first thing tomorrow morning we will set off for Moab. Maybe there will be more food there.'

It was a big upheaval for the whole family to leave their home and travel to a foreign country. Apart from anything else, the people in Moab didn't like the Israelites. And of course, it was a long way to travel by foot—or even by donkey. Now whether it was a result of the travelling or not, we don't know, but soon after their arrival, Elimelech died. Naomi and her two sons were left alone in a hostile foreign land. However, Naomi knew that whatever happened and wherever they were, God would always be with them.

'Mum, I'm going to get married!' Mahlon told his mother in great excitement one day. 'I've met a wonderful Moabite girl.'

Naomi didn't know whether to be joyful or sad. She'd always hoped that her two sons would marry Israelite girls.

'Be happy for me, Mum,' Mahlon pleaded, looking deeply into his mother's eyes. 'It will be all right, you'll see!'

Naomi sensed that Mahlon had gone a bit silly—the way people do when they're in love. He seemed to spend the next few weeks writing love letters and picking flowers for his beloved. That being the situation, and after realizing that there were no Israelite girls living in that area anyway, Naomi reluctantly gave her consent.

It wasn't long before both the boys were married to Moabite girls. Their names were Orpah and Ruth. They were good marriages, but after a few years, Mahlon and Chilion both died suddenly. Naomi was really distraught. All she wanted to do was to go back to her people in Israel.

Reproduced with permission from *Stories to Read Aloud* published by BRF 2004 (1 84101 362 5)

At last, the news reached Moab that there was food in Israel again. Naomi began to pack her bags to return to her own people after ten years in Moab. She was a sad and broken woman, having lost her husband and both sons.

As she prepared to leave her home in Moab, Naomi hugged her two daughters-in-law, saying, 'You have been good to my boys and me. Now the time has come for me to return to my homeland, and you must go back to your people.'

Orpah made her way back to her family in Moab without too much persuasion, but Ruth refused to leave Naomi.

'I'm not leaving you,' she told Naomi, with determination and commitment. 'I will never leave you. Wherever you go, I will go,' she continued. 'Where you live, I will live. I will accept your people as my people, and I will even worship your God.'

Naomi was quite taken aback by Ruth's love and commitment to her, realizing that she meant every word.

'Come along, then,' Naomi said, as she smiled and took Ruth's arm. 'We've got a long way to go.'

As the couple travelled back to Israel, they talked together. Having left Israel with hopes of a new start, Naomi was sad to be returning with no husband and no sons.

Though Ruth felt tremendous compassion for her mother-in-law, at the same time she was wondering what lay ahead for both of them.

'Maybe I will find romance in Israel,' she muttered quietly to herself, and grinned secretly. Maybe she will!·

Reproduced with permission from *Stories to Read Aloud* published by BRF 2004 (1 84101 362 5)

14

The generosity of love

Teacher's information

Bible reference

The story is based on Ruth 2:1—4:22.

Theme

In order to free Ruth to marry him, Boaz has to buy all the family's land. In this case, that means the land which had belonged to Elimelech and his two sons.

Key verses

Boaz told the town leaders and everyone else: All of you are witnesses that today I have bought from Naomi the property that belonged to Elimelech and his two sons, Chilion and Mahlon. You are also witnesses that I have agreed to marry Mahlon's widow Ruth, the Moabite woman. This will keep the property in his family's name, and he will be remembered in this town.
RUTH 4:9–10

Talk about…

What we could give to enable others to be free.

Aim

To understand the generosity of Jesus' love when he gave his life on the cross for us so that we could be freed from the consequences of our wrong-doing and be reunited with God.

Jigsaw puzzled

Dear God…
You must love us a lot to have sent your Son Jesus to die on the cross for us.

Activitime

Using a Bible, compare 1 John 3:16 with John 3:16.

Jigsaw piece

The significance of this Old Testament story lies not just in the spiritual messages contained but in the fact that Ruth and Boaz were ancestors of King David. Because Jesus was to be born into an earthly family who were descended from David, this whole relationship is quite significant.

Prayback

Our loving God,
Thank you that you had an important plan for Boaz's and Ruth's lives, which was fulfilled through Boaz's love. Thank you that you love us so much that you sent your Son, Jesus, to live in the world. Thank you that he loved us so much that he died on the cross for us. Thank you that he rose from the dead and is alive today. Thank you that your love is so generous.
Please help us to love one another. In Jesus' name. Amen

A story of true love (Part Two)

Last time, we left Ruth and Naomi on their way back to Israel. Naomi was a sad and broken woman, but Ruth was determined to support her good friend. Perhaps she was also hoping for a bit of romance in her life. Both Ruth and Naomi realized that life wasn't going to be easy on their return, but they had decided to make the best of it.

The law in Israel at the time stated that poor people could go into the fields after the harvest had been gathered by the farmer. They could collect up any of the crop that was left. So when Ruth and Naomi arrived at their destination, Ruth decided that she would go out and do just that.

Now it so happened that she found herself in a field belonging to one of her husband's relatives—although perhaps it wasn't just coincidence. The man's name was Boaz. He arrived at the field where Ruth was collecting grain on that particular day. It was a wonderful moment when their eyes met. Ruth stared at Boaz—he was strong and handsome—and Boaz was dazzled by Ruth's beauty and her kind face.

'Who's the young lady over there?' Boaz asked the foreman, blushing slightly.

'She's pretty, isn't she?' the foreman replied, grinning from ear to ear. 'That's the young widow who came back with Naomi from Moab.'

Boaz walked over to where Ruth was working, feeling very flushed, his heart pounding. He gave a little cough—not that he needed to attract her attention, because she hadn't taken her eyes off him for one moment.

'You're very welcome to continue to gather grain in my field,' he said nervously. 'And if you're thirsty, do help yourself to a drink from over there.'

Boaz pointed to where the water was. Ruth turned away and grinned shyly. It was the first time she'd heard anyone use that as a chat-up line.

'I don't know what I've done to deserve your kindness,' she replied.

But news had travelled fast. Boaz knew all about the way that Ruth was standing by Naomi.

At lunchtime, Boaz invited Ruth to come over and have something to eat with him. It was roasted grain. She didn't eat much—she was too much in love! After they had eaten, Boaz told his harvesters to leave a little bit of extra grain behind for Ruth to gather, so by the end of the day she had quite a lot to take home.

'Good day in the fields?' Naomi enquired, when Ruth arrived home.

'Fine,' she replied, trying not to give anything away.

Naomi detected a twinkle in Ruth's eye. The young woman was all bouncy and had a 'miles away' look about her.

'Anything to tell me?' Naomi asked, fishing

Reproduced with permission from *Stories to Read Aloud* published by BRF 2004 (1 84101 362 5)

for information—just as parents do.

'Well,' Ruth answered, pausing for a moment, not knowing whether to say anything or not. 'Well,' she repeated, 'I was gathering grain from Boaz's field and he was very polite and generous.'

'Do I detect a bit of romance in the air?' Naomi asked, knowingly.

Ruth smiled a smile that gave everything away—she had fallen madly in love with the young man.

'Ruth's got a boyfriend!' Naomi chanted repeatedly, as she did a little dance around the room—that is, until she felt her knee almost give way underneath her.

'Oh dear,' she said, 'I'm forgetting my age in all the excitement.'

With that, Naomi sank down into a chair. Naomi signalled for Ruth to sit down as well, while she regained her breath.

'Right now, stop wasting time,' Naomi told Ruth. 'We must work quickly. Go to Boaz in the barn, lie down near him and ask him if you can share his cover. That will be a sign to him that you want to marry him.'

So Ruth did as Naomi had told her. Boaz was a little surprised, but delighted to think that Ruth wanted to be his wife. However, to free her to marry him, Boaz had to buy the land that belonged to Elimelech's family. It was the custom in those parts and times that to marry a widow you had to buy the family's land. Equally, if you wanted to buy the family's land, you had to marry the widow—and close relatives had first refusal.

Talking of close relatives, there happened to be a closer relative than Boaz, who had to be given the first opportunity to buy the land and marry Ruth if he wanted to. So Boaz decided to go and see him.

Good news! It turned out that though the other man wanted to buy the field, he didn't want to marry Ruth. So Boaz bought the family land, thus paying the price to free Ruth to marry him.

Boaz's act of generosity, stemming from his love for Ruth, set her free to enter into a wonderful relationship with him. They got married and, as far as we know, they lived happily ever after.

15

God knows our true potential

 Bible reference

The story is based on 1 Samuel 16:1–13.

 Theme

God's choice of king is based on much more than just outward appearances.

 Key verse

But the Lord told him, 'Samuel, don't think Eliab is the one just because he's tall and handsome. He isn't the one I've chosen. People judge others by what they look like, but I judge people by what is in their hearts.'
1 SAMUEL 16:7

 Talk about…

What the word 'potential' means.

 Aim

Not to judge people by outward appearances.

Jigsaw puzzled

Dear God…
How important are looks?

 Activitime

On a piece of paper, write down something good about the person sitting next to you—but nothing to do with their appearance. After you have written it down, give it to them as an encouragement.

 Jigsaw piece

After the Israelites had settled into the promised land of Canaan, the time came when they wanted to be like other nations and have a king. Saul, the first king, disobeys God, so a new king has to be found.

Prayback

God who knows our hearts,
    Thank you that you do not judge us on our outward appearances. Please help us not to judge other people by the way they look. Thank you that you equip us to do the things that you have chosen us to do for you. Please help us to be prepared to do those things. In Jesus' name. Amen

Tall, dark and handsome

In Old Testament times, when a new king was chosen by God, he would have a few drops of oil poured on to his head from a hollow ram's horn. It was called 'anointing', and was a sign of being chosen by God. Well, one day, God spoke to his servant Samuel concerning the selection of someone to replace King Saul, because King Saul had disobeyed God.

'Cheer up, Samuel,' God said. 'You mustn't keep thinking about Saul—we've got work to do. Now, fill up a ram's horn with oil and get yourself ready to travel. You're off to Bethlehem. I've decided that one of Jesse's sons will be the new king.'

'Is it wise for me to do that?' Samuel asked, more than a little nervous. 'What if Saul finds out what's going on? After all, he is still king at the moment. He might kill me.'

'Oh, you worry too much for your own good, Samuel,' God replied reassuringly. 'All you need to do is take a young cow with you to sacrifice at Jesse's. What better reason to be there? And while you're there, you can anoint the son that I have chosen.'

Samuel did just as God had told him. When he arrived at Bethlehem, a group of officials from the town came to meet him. Samuel was sweating a bit, through nerves, but he needn't have worried, because the officials were more frightened about him than he was about them.

'What are you here for? Is it peaceful?' they asked.

'Don't panic,' Samuel smiled, with some relief. 'I'm here to give thanks to God. Why don't you come and join me?'

The little party made their way to Jesse's house. Samuel explained the whole situation and they gave thanks to God.

While he was there, Samuel began to look around at Jesse's sons and wonder which one God wanted to be king. Then he spotted Eliab. He was tall, very good-looking and rippling with muscles, and he had a wonderful smile. He looked like a world champion athlete.

'This has got to be the one,' Samuel whispered to himself quietly but confidently.

No one heard what he had said—except God, that is.

Reproduced with permission from *Stories to Read Aloud* published by BRF 2004 (1 84101 362 5)

'Sorry, Samuel,' God said emphatically. 'This is not the one. He's a fine figure of a man, but I judge on what's inside, not on the outward appearance.'

'I'm afraid that God has rejected your eldest son,' Samuel told Jesse. 'Who's next?'

One by one, Jesse's sons passed in front of Samuel—Abinadab, then Shammah... After seven of Jesse's sons had made an appearance, poor Samuel was confused.

'I just don't understand it,' he said nervously to Jesse. 'God hasn't chosen any of the lads that I've seen. I know it's a silly question, but are you sure that you haven't got any more sons?'

Samuel felt a bit silly saying such a thing, so he was quite pleased when Jesse replied that he had.

'Well, there is young David,' he chuckled, 'but he's only a shepherd boy. He could never be king.'

'Nevertheless, I must see him,' Samuel answered.

'As you wish,' Jesse replied reluctantly, and he sent his servant off to fetch the boy.

Everyone chatted among themselves while they waited. Samuel felt a little self-conscious—almost as if people expected him to tell some jokes or sing a solo in the meantime, but he didn't!

'This is the one,' God told Samuel as soon as the lad arrived.

Samuel was so pleased. He had the same kind of feeling that you might get when you hear that you have just passed all your GCSE exams—a mixture of joy and relief. Anyway, David was anointed and from that time God began to prepare him for the job that he was going to do.

So you see, God doesn't judge us on our looks. He judges us on what we are like on the inside. Even if we're not outwardly beautiful or handsome, we can still have a wonderful personality, be loving, kind, generous and thoughtful, and be useful and obedient to God.

Oh yes! And when God chooses us to do a particular job for him, he always equips us to do it.

Reproduced with permission from *Stories to Read Aloud* published by BRF 2004 (1 84101 362 5)

16

True wisdom is a gift from God

Teacher's information

 Bible reference

The story is based on 1 Kings 2:1—11:43.

 Theme

Solomon realizes what a responsibility it is to be king, so he asks God to equip him to make wise decisions.

 Key verse

'Please make me wise and teach me the difference between right and wrong. Then I will know how to rule your people. If you don't, there is no way I could rule this great nation of yours.'
1 KINGS 3:9

 Talk about...

How wisdom differs from knowledge.

 Aim

To look to God for the right thing to do in a situation, and do it!

Jigsaw puzzled

Dear God...
Can you help me to make wise decisions?

 Activitime

Have a short general knowledge quiz. Questions might include:

*   What is the name of our present Prime Minister?
*   Where is the Queen's Norfolk residence?
*   What do the letters RSPCA stand for?

Jigsaw piece

Solomon was King David's son and reigned over the Israelites as king, following David's death. In this story, Solomon asks God for the gift of wisdom.

Prayback

Generous God,
Thank you that you are wise, and that you give wisdom to those who ask for it. Please help us to acquire knowledge from the Bible, and grant us the wisdom to apply it to the situations that we meet each day. And fill those in positions of authority and responsibility with wisdom to do their jobs well and according to your standards. In Jesus' name. Amen

I'd like to be wise

It's a big responsibility being king. It was especially so in Old Testament times, because the king had a lot of authority in those days. He had to rule, carry out justice, go into battle, provide for the poor, protect the vulnerable… in fact, he had to do many, many things. It wasn't just a case of walking about the palace wearing an expensive crown.

When Solomon became king of Israel, he had to do all the things that kings normally did—and as if that wasn't enough, he was to be responsible for building a temple as well. A temple is a kind of big church.

'As if it isn't bad enough coping with my father David's death, to have all the responsibilities of being king thrust on to me as well… How will I cope?' Solomon mumbled to himself despairingly.

Then he remembered the old king's faithfulness to God and his parting words: 'Always listen to God, and do what he tells you to do!'

So Solomon decided to pray and ask for help. Realizing his own weakness, he asked God to give him wisdom for his position as king, to help him to know what to do in every situation, particularly the tough ones—talking of which…

One day, Solomon was sitting on his throne, wearing his sparkly crown and holding his ornate jewelled golden sceptre—or whatever kings do in their spare time—when suddenly there was a hullabaloo outside the door. It sounded like a bull in a china shop!

'Whatever is going on?' Solomon shouted to one of his servant girls, trying to be heard above the noise.

'There are two rather cross ladies arguing in the hallway, Your Majesty,' she replied, curtsying. 'And they're not really the sort of ladies we want in the palace, either.'

'In what way?' Solomon enquired.

'Well, they're rather rough, badly behaved ladies,' she replied tactfully.

Suddenly, the door burst open and the two ladies almost fell into the room. They certainly looked very rough, as they shouted at each other. Then the punches started to fly, although one of the ladies seemed to be having difficulty hitting the other, because she had a strange-looking bundle under her arm.

'Excuse me!' screamed the king in a very loud voice.

The room went silent, except for the whimpering of a baby.

'Where's that noise coming from?' the king asked, looking around in confusion.

'Oh, that's my baby,' answered the lady with the bundle under her arm. She unwrapped the package to reveal a very young baby. She put him on the floor. He seemed surprisingly contented under the circumstances.

'He's not yours, he's mine,' the other lady shouted, grabbing at him.

With that, the arguing and fighting began again.

Well, it turned out that both the ladies had

Reproduced with permission from *Stories to Read Aloud* published by BRF 2004 (1 84101 362 5)

had babies, but one had died. The dead baby's mother had swapped the babies while the other mother had been asleep, and the result was that each of the two ladies was claiming that the live baby belonged to her.

King Solomon had got the job of sorting out who was the real mother.

'Rather you than me!' one of the king's advisers said, laughing nervously.

'All right,' the king said, 'lay the baby on the table here.'

The baby was placed on to the table and the king asked for a sword to be brought. He made a few quick calculations to find where the middle of the baby was, drew a cross on the baby's clothes in the appropriate place and proudly announced that the baby would be cut in half. Then the two mums could have half each.

Under Solomon's instruction, a servant raised the heavy, sharp sword until it was ready to swing down towards the baby.

'On the count of three,' Solomon said confidently. 'One! Two! ...'

The sword was just about to come down on the baby when...

'STOP!!!!!' one of the ladies shouted. 'Give the baby to the other mum. At least he will still live.'

Solomon knew immediately that the lady who had stopped him from killing the baby was the real mother.

'Give the baby to her,' he commanded the servant girl, pointing to the lady who had saved the baby's life. 'She's the real mother.'

Having watched the dispute being sorted out, the servant girl bustled the women out.

'I thought that you really were going to have the baby killed,' the king's adviser laughed. 'I wouldn't have dared to do it. How did you know that the real mother would stop it?'

'Obvious, my man. Of course the real mother would protect her child—even if it meant giving him up to someone else,' the king replied, with a satisfied grin on his face.

Unfortunately, though Solomon had been gifted with wisdom from God, he didn't always act on it. During his reign, he did a lot of good, besides building the temple. But he also encouraged the Israelites to worship false gods made of wood, stone and precious metals—and that was not good. You see, the Israelites' loyalties became split. As they worshipped the false gods, they turned their backs on the one true God—the God who had been so good to the old king and had given Solomon great wisdom.

It's one thing to have great wisdom from God, but wisdom is no good if we do not act upon it.

Reproduced with permission from *Stories to Read Aloud* published by BRF 2004 (1 84101 362 5)

17

God's daily provision for us

Teacher's information

 ### Bible reference

The story is based on 1 Kings 17:7–24.

 ### Theme

God promises to provide for Elijah and his hosts until the rain comes again.

 ### Key verse

'The Lord God of Israel has promised that your jar of flour won't run out and your bottle of oil won't dry up before he sends rain for the crops.'
1 KINGS 17:14

 ### Talk about…

The fact that although we plant and harvest, we still need God to bring growth.

 ### Aim

To appreciate and share the things that God provides for us.

Jigsaw puzzled

Dear God…
If we shared more, not so many people would go short, would they?

 ### Activitime

Have a bring-and-share feast. Everyone brings something to eat that can be shared with the rest of the group. **NB:** To ensure safety, make sure that you know beforehand of any food allergies that the children might have.

 ### Jigsaw piece

Elijah was an Old Testament prophet of God. To put it simply, it was his job to tell the Israelites all about God and his plans—and to let them know when God was angry! After Elijah told Ahab, one of the kings of Israel, that God was going to bring a drought, God told Elijah to go into hiding at the Cherith ravine. But he soon discovers that it is not quite the holiday that he expected.

Prayback

Our loving heavenly Father,
Thank you for all that you provide for us, for natural resources and the ability to make use of them, for the seasons, the sunshine and the rain, and for the ability to plant and the gift of growth. Please help us not to be greedy. Teach us to share what we have with those who have less than we do. In Jesus' name. Amen

The last meal

When Elijah first arrived at the Cherith ravine, he quite enjoyed the peace and quiet. It was a good opportunity to catch up with some serious sunbathing. The flies were a bit of a nuisance at first, but he made himself a makeshift swatter with some large leaves that were growing nearby. There were squashed flies everywhere!

It was a great way of life… that is, until the nearby brook dried up owing to lack of rain. Then it was a different story.

'Just as I was enjoying myself,' Elijah groaned—although, if the truth be known, he was beginning to feel a little bit lonely.

Anyway, Elijah did what he always did when he had problems. He knelt down and asked God what he should do.

'It's time to make a move,' God told him. 'Go to Zarephath! There's a very kind widow there who will provide you with a room to stay in and food and drink.'

Elijah quickly converted his makeshift fly-swatter into a makeshift sunhat, ready for the long walk to Zarephath. It was a hot journey, but he made it safely to the town gate, where he spotted a lady gathering some firewood. Elijah associated firewood with cooking, because they used to cook over wood fires in those days.

'This must be the widow I'm looking for,' he thought.

'Any chance of a drink for a weary traveller?' Elijah asked her. 'Please?'

The lady didn't say anything—she just began to draw some water from the well for him.

'And a piece of bread to go with it would be nice,' he continued. 'Please?'

Can you believe that anyone would be so cheeky as to go up to a complete stranger and ask for bread and water—even though God had arranged everything beforehand? Well, at Elijah's second request, the widow turned round rather sharply.

'And I suppose you want jam on it as well,' she snapped—or words to that effect.

You see, she was a little touchy about the food situation. Owing to the lack of rain there to make the crops grow, she only had enough flour and oil left to make one final meal for herself and her son. After explaining that to Elijah, she said very bluntly, 'And then we'll die!'

Elijah smiled.

'Cook me some bread first. Then you can cook a meal for yourselves,' he told the lady. Selfish, or what? Not really, because at the same time Elijah passed on a wonderful promise to the widow and her son.

'God has promised that, until the rain comes again, the jar where you keep your flour and the jug where you keep oil will never be empty. Both will be refilled quite miraculously, as quickly as you use what is in them.'

How's that for a dream come true? The lady

smiled a smile of disbelief, but decided to make Elijah a meal, anyway. She thought he'd got a good sense of humour, for a stranger.

However, sure enough, whenever the widow had made some bread, she would return to the containers later and each time they would be full again. She got so excited every time it happened.

Sadly, the excitement was soon lost when her son died suddenly. 'It's all your fault!' she shouted at Elijah.

Poor Elijah was a little taken aback by that, but he very calmly took the boy's body and said, 'Leave it to me.'

Elijah took the boy to another room and laid him down. What was he to do? It's all very well saying, 'Leave it to me' when someone has died.

'Only one thing to do,' Elijah mumbled to himself.

'I need your help, God,' he shouted out, as he began to pray harder than ever before. 'God, please let this boy live,' Elijah asked repeatedly. 'His mum has been so good to me, and now she blames me for this happening.'

In the middle of the prayer, Elijah suddenly heard a faint voice asking, 'What's for tea, Mum? I'm so hungry! I could eat a mountain lion.'

Elijah sank into the armchair, sweat pouring off his forehead.

'Thanks, God!' he shouted, relieved and very pleased. The boy was alive! 'Let's take you down to your mother,' Elijah told him.

The poor widow couldn't believe her eyes. For a moment, she was absolutely speechless. Then she shouted at the top of her voice, 'He's alive!'

After tea, she turned to Elijah and gave him a big wet kiss on the cheek.

'You really are a friend of God, aren't you?' she said.

He nodded.

'And what you say really is the truth?'

He nodded again.

'I can tell,' she continued, 'because I have seen the power of God at work through you— God's servant.'

Reproduced with permission from *Stories to Read Aloud* published by BRF 2004 (1 84101 362 5)

18

There is only one true God

Teacher's information

 ### Bible reference

The story is based on 1 Kings 18:1–40.

 ### Theme

The result of the contest is that the God of Elijah is the one 'true' God.

 ### Key verse

The Lord immediately sent fire, and it burnt up the sacrifice, the wood, and the stones. It scorched the ground everywhere around the altar and dried up every drop of water in the ditch.
1 KINGS 18:38

 ### Talk about…

False gods that people worship today—things that take first place in our lives, such as TV, drugs, money, possessions and so on.

 ### Aim

To put God first in our lives.

Jigsaw puzzled

Dear God…
Is it all right to worship more than one god?

 ### Activitime

Our society is very money- and possession-orientated. Cut out some pictures from newspapers or magazines and make a collage to represent that.

 ### Jigsaw piece

A lot happened after God had led the Israelites from Egypt, through the wilderness, to the promised land of Canaan—not all of it good. One of the bad things that happened was that the Israelites started to worship statues as if they were gods, instead of the God of the Bible. That made God angry.

Prayback

Almighty God,
Thank you that you are a powerful God and the one true God. Please help us to worship only you and not be tempted to worship money, possessions, or anything similar. Enable our society today to recognize you as the true and powerful God that you are. In Jesus' name. Amen

How not to prepare a bonfire

It was, perhaps, the game show to beat all game shows. It certainly brought in the crowds, anyway. All the Israelites were there in force. Many had brought their packed lunches and were all set to make a day of it. They spread their cloaks on the ground and sat down, ready to be entertained.

'Has Elijah arrived yet?' someone shouted across the crowd.

The question was heard echoing in the valleys around… 'yet… yet… yet… yet!' Then suddenly there was a very loud but rather mocking cheer. Elijah was walking up the slope towards the crowd.

'Hey, look, here comes the old misery!' one of the Israelites shouted. And everyone laughed.

The laughter sounded like gurgling drains. It could be heard across the hillside. Elijah didn't mind, though—he knew that they were all in for a surprise.

Elijah was a prophet of God. To put it simply, it was his job to tell the Israelites all about God and his plans—and let them know when God was not pleased. Talking of which… Elijah had been concerned because the Israelites thought that they could worship both God *and* false gods such as Baal. God definitely was not pleased!

As a result, Elijah had challenged the people to make a choice—to follow either God or Baal, not both. To help them to decide between the two, a contest had been arranged, to take place on Mount Carmel, between Elijah and 450 prophets of Baal. Four hundred prophets of Asherah were invited along, too. This would prove who was the most powerful—the God of Elijah, or Baal.

The plan was that Elijah would set up a sort of bonfire on which he would place some meat that had been prepared as an offering. He then had to light the bonfire just by praying. If it had been today, he would not have been allowed to use matches or anything like that. In fact, he wasn't even allowed to go near it. The prophets of Baal had to do the same.

'You start,' Elijah said to his opponents, with a smile on his face.

Reproduced with permission from *Stories to Read Aloud* published by BRF 2004 (1 84101 362 5)

So the prophets of Baal began work. They built the fire, prepared the meat, and started praying. They began praying in the morning, and were still praying—unsuccessfully—at lunchtime.

'Oh, come on, Baal,' they pleaded. 'Give us a light.'

But nothing happened. In the evening, they were still praying hard, but nothing had happened. They even tried cutting themselves with swords and—surprise, surprise—that didn't help either. The prophets of Baal felt rather cross and very silly.

'Can I warm my toes by your fire?' Elijah joked.

His opponents frowned and stamped their feet in frustration.

'It's my turn now,' Elijah called, 'but, first of all, pour some water over my bonfire.'

Obediently, some of the people ran forward to do as Elijah had asked. In fact, they did it quite willingly. 'He's crazy,' they thought. They didn't believe that Elijah's God could set fire to the wood when it was dry, let alone when it was wet.

'Pour some more water on,' Elijah told them.

Willingly, they splashed water all over the wood once again.

'Once more, if you please,' Elijah requested very politely.

The onlookers couldn't keep straight faces now. Some of them were rolling on the floor, tears running down their cheeks. More water was poured on to the now-sodden firewood.

'This we've got to see,' they all cackled together, like a pack of hyenas.

I know I said that it was like a game show, but in reality it was a very serious challenge with important consequences. The issue at stake was to prove to the people of Israel that God was the one true God and that all the other gods, like Baal, were false. By soaking the bonfire with water, Elijah really was going to demonstrate that God can do the impossible.

Elijah knelt down and prayed to God.

'Show them that you are the one true God,' he said. 'Wipe the smiles off their faces by demonstrating your power.'

Suddenly, the bonfire, running in water, burst into flames. It was like fireworks night… and more! Everything was burned up—the wood, the meat, even the stones that Elijah had put round the wood, and all the water.

Well, when everyone saw what had happened, they didn't say much. They just got on their knees and believed in and worshipped the God of Elijah—the one true God.

19

The faithfulness of God

Teacher's information

Bible reference

The story is based on Daniel 3:1–30.

Theme

God prevents any harm coming to the three men in the fiery furnace.

Key verse

'But I see four men walking around in the fire,' the king replied. 'None of them is tied up or harmed, and the fourth one looks like a god.'
DANIEL 3:25

Talk about…

People whom we trust.

Aim

To trust God because he is faithful.

Jigsaw puzzled

Dear God…
Whom can we really trust?

Activitime

Draw a picture of someone we trust and write a list below the picture of why we trust them.

Jigsaw piece

During King Nebuchadnezzar's reign in Babylon, the Babylonians attacked Jerusalem and took many hostages back to Babylon. The three characters in this story are three of the hostages who were taken. The place is Babylon.

Prayback

Eternal God,
Thank you that you are a faithful God, whom we can depend on. Please help us to trust you more. In Jesus' name. Amen

Hot, hot, hot

'Well, what do you think?' King Nebuchadnezzar shouted, as he pointed to the new golden statue he had commissioned to be built.

'It's very high, Your Majesty,' one of the king's officials replied nervously. 'It seems to disappear into the clouds.'

'Of course it's very high. It is a symbol of my power and authority,' Nebuchadnezzar thundered.

Another of the officials, who was a little weary of saying the wrong thing, just said, 'It's very "gold", isn't it?'

The chancellor said, in a quiet whisper behind the king's back so that he didn't hear, 'It's very expensive!'

King Nebuchadnezzar had called together all the officials of the land to see the new monument. Everyone stood in awe as they looked up into the clouds. Then the herald began to speak.

'Listen carefully to what I have to say. At great expense, the king's dance band have learned to play a new tune. You can't miss it, because of the wonderful harp solo in the middle. Whenever you hear it played at the base of this statue, everyone must fall down and worship this wonderful monument to the king.'

One or two folk began to whisper.

'You won't catch me getting my knees dirty,' one laughed.

'Anyone who does not follow the king's instructions will be thrown into a blazing furnace,' the herald continued. 'A very, very, very hot one!'

Everyone swallowed hard, especially the ones who had been whispering together. They could feel the sweat running down their backs already.

Now there were three Jewish lads living in the land who believed, quite rightly, that they should only worship the one true God. So when the music played, they didn't follow King Nebuchadnezzar's instructions. This could have gone unnoticed if it hadn't been for a handful of folk who were jealous of the

Reproduced with permission from *Stories to Read Aloud* published by BRF 2004 (1 84101 362 5)

three boys' positions. These people 'just had to' inform the king.

When the informers were summoned into court, one of the men edged forward nervously.

'O mighty King, Your Highness, Your Majesty…'

'Oh, do stop grovelling,' roared the king angrily. 'What do you want?'

A long explanation followed, including the names Shadrach, Meshach and Abednego. King Nebuchadnezzar was furious. He summoned the three to question them. But they still refused to obey his orders.

'You know what will happen if you continue with this attitude,' Nebuchadnezzar threatened.

'Your threats don't bother us,' Shadrach, Meshach and Abednego replied together. 'If you throw us into the flames, our God can protect us. We have nothing to fear from you.'

The king turned white with anger. He banged his fist down on the table so hard that the whole room echoed.

'Mind the table,' one of the servants mumbled. But fortunately, the king's mind was on other things, so he didn't hear.

The king turned to his guards. 'Heat up the furnace. Make it hotter than ever before. Tie these traitors up and throw them into the flames. Make them scream!' he said cruelly.

Sure enough, King Nebuchadnezzar's orders were carried out to the letter and he was there to watch. The flames were so hot that the soldiers who threw the men into the fire were killed by the heat. Then suddenly, Nebuchadnezzar leapt to his feet and shouted out.

'This can't be happening! Look, look, look! There are four men in the furnace, unbound, unharmed and walking around in the flames.'

The king ran to the opening of the furnace and called the men to come out. Shadrach, Meshach and Abednego came out untouched by the fire, although sweating a little, and leaving a trail of sooty footprints on the ground. The king fell down and worshipped God.

On that occasion, God demonstrated his tremendous power and faithfulness. We're not told who the fourth person was—it could have been an angel, or it could have been Jesus. Certainly, it was someone who had been sent by God to protect those three lads—and that's exactly what he did!

Reproduced with permission from *Stories to Read Aloud* published by BRF 2004 (1 84101 362 5)

20

Courage to do what is right, in the face of opposition

Teacher's information

Bible reference

The story is based on Daniel 6:1–28.

Theme

Despite the king's decree, Daniel continues to do the right thing—praying to God.

Key verse

Daniel heard about the law, but when he returned home, he went upstairs and prayed in front of the window that faced Jerusalem. In the same way that he had always done, he knelt down in prayer three times a day, giving thanks to God.

DANIEL 6:10

Talk about...

When it could be hard for us to do the right thing.

Aim

We should be prepared to stand alone for God when necessary.

Jigsaw puzzled

Dear God…
Should I do what you want me to do even when other people are making fun of me?

Activitime

Make a notice for a lions' enclosure in an imaginary zoo or wildlife park, highlighting the danger of lions. Start it with the words, 'Do not climb over the safety fence because…' (Appropriate serious or humorous illustrations can be used.)

Jigsaw piece

This story concerns Daniel, another of the Jewish hostages who were taken to Babylon. He too followed God.

Prayback

Precious God,
Thank you for this wonderful story of courage—that Daniel was prepared to risk his life in the lions' enclosure in order to stand up for what he knew to be right. Please help us to follow his example. Give us the courage to do the things that we know you would have us do, even when our friends, family, society or the media seem to say the opposite. In Jesus' name. Amen

Lunchtime

The lions prowled round their large enclosure, roaring menacingly, with their huge teeth displayed for all to see. They looked as if they hadn't eaten for a while. Their keeper watched. He was a sinister-looking man, who revelled in watching his 'pussy cats' devouring raw meat.

'Getting hungry, my beauties?' he asked the beasts, as he smiled and rubbed his hands. 'Don't worry,' he continued. 'Soon you will have a nice piece of human flesh to eat.'

With that, he burst into fits of spine-chilling laughter.

Daniel, a young Jewish lad who had been taken into exile by the Babylonians, was to be thrown to the hungry lions at any moment, much to the distress of King Darius. You see, poor foolish Darius had been tricked by some of the people in his government, and Daniel's awful fate was the result.

Let me start at the beginning. When Daniel was taken into exile, he proved to be honest, reliable and responsible. God was with him, so he did well and was given a position of great responsibility.

The time came when King Darius planned to put Daniel in charge of the whole kingdom, and that displeased some of the ambitious members of the government.

So, one day, Daniel's enemies got together to discuss the situation. They huddled into a scrum-like formation, in a quiet corner. They looked just like a group of rugby players— except a lot cleaner and more puny.

'Let's make a plan to get rid of Daniel,' one of them suggested.

'We could burn his house down when he's asleep in bed,' another added.

'No, no, no, we need to be more cunning than that,' another schemed. 'We need to find a weakness, something that he's done wrong, which we can report to the king.'

The men talked and plotted for hours, but could find no fault in Daniel. Then suddenly, one of them shouted out.

'I've got it!' he yelled. 'What does Daniel do three times a day? He prays to his God! The

Reproduced with permission from *Stories to Read Aloud* published by BRF 2004 (1 84101 362 5)

king is arrogant and a little foolish. All we need to do is get him to bring out a new decree. It will say that anyone who prays to any god or man apart from him in the next thirty days will be thrown to the lions.'

'Yes!' they all shouted in unison, and they ran about waving their arms in the air and hugging each other, just as footballers do when they have scored a goal.

Sure enough, the king fell right into the trap.

'No one will stop me from speaking to my God in prayer,' Daniel said courageously when he heard of the new law. He kept praying to God three times a day, near his window.

The plotters reported it to the king, so Daniel was sentenced to be thrown to the lions—hence the hungry lions waiting for some human flesh.

Poor Darius was so upset, because he liked Daniel. But there was no way out without looking foolish. By the time the sun began to set, the king realized that the punishment had to be carried out. As Daniel was led to the lions' den, Darius grabbed his arm.

'I'm so sorry, Daniel,' he wept. 'I was tricked. Your only hope now is that your God will rescue you.'

Daniel smiled and boldly walked into the enclosure. A large stone was hastily rolled across the entrance.

That night, the king couldn't eat or sleep. As soon as it was light again, he rushed out to see if Daniel was still alive. At first, he couldn't see his friend. Then suddenly, from among the sleeping lions came a familiar voice.

'Are you looking for me?' Daniel asked, as he stood up and brushed the hairs off his coat.

There was not even a scratch on him. The king was overjoyed. Daniel scrambled over the lions, making his way to the entrance where King Darius waited excitedly.

'I should be cross with you,' Daniel told him, smiling, 'but I'm not.'

Daniel was released and the evil plotters were fed to the hungry lions instead.

'I'm going to write a new decree,' King Darius announced to Daniel after it was all over. 'I'm going to command everyone to treat your God with great respect and worship him as the living God.'

Daniel had shown great courage in order to do what he knew to be right, even though it had meant standing alone for God. Daniel's actions and God's response had a tremendous effect on the whole of the community: everyone learned a lot more about God.

Reproduced with permission from *Stories to Read Aloud* published by BRF 2004 (1 84101 362 5)

God is a God of love and forgiveness

Teacher's information

 ### Bible reference

The story is based on Jonah 1:1—4:11.

 ### Theme

God forgives the people of Nineveh because they are really sorry for the things that they have done wrong.

 ### Key verse

When God saw that the people had stopped doing evil things, he had pity and did not destroy them as he had planned.
JONAH 3:10

 ### Talk about...

Times when other people do things to hurt or upset us.

 ### Aim

To forgive other people.

Jigsaw puzzled

Dear God...
Should we seek revenge or forgive?

 ### Activitime

Write a postcard to an imaginary friend whom you have fallen out with, aiming to mend the broken relationship.

Jigsaw piece

This story comes towards the end of the Old Testament. At the time when this incident takes place, Nineveh is the capital of Assyria, a nation that is an enemy to the Israelites. The idea that God could forgive the enemies of his chosen people is unthinkable to the Israelites. However, God's forgiveness is available to all nations.

Prayback

Loving Father,
Thank you that you are a God of forgiveness and that your forgiveness is available to everyone. Please help us to forgive other people who have done things to upset or hurt us. In Jesus' name. Amen

No escape!

Once upon a time, there was a man called Jonah. He was what, in those days, would be called a 'God-fearing man'. I don't mean that he was afraid of God, but that he recognized the power and authority of God and lived according to his laws. Mind you, Jonah was soon to learn a lot more about God in a very unexpected way.

Jonah was having a lie-in on this particular morning, when suddenly he heard a loud voice.

'Jonah, I've got a job for you!' the voice echoed through the house.

Jonah put his fingers in his ears, trying to get back to sleep. But the voice wouldn't go away. Eventually, Jonah reluctantly rolled out of bed. Not realizing who was speaking to him, he went to the front door, but, to his surprise, there was nobody there.

'Must be someone at the window,' he mumbled to himself.

But there was nobody at any of the windows, either. Then, just as Jonah was about to go back to bed, he heard the voice again.

'Jonah, it's me, God. I want you to go to Nineveh, because I have a message for the people there.'

Jonah was quick to reply.

'Sorry!' he told God. 'I don't really feel called to that sort of work. Besides, I've got a very busy day today.'

Jonah went back to bed, but he couldn't seem to get to sleep again, because he kept thinking about what had just happened.

'I think I got away with it,' he said to himself. But to be on the safe side, he felt that perhaps he should run away. Tarshish was in the opposite direction to Nineveh. Surely God wouldn't be able to reach him there!

Hastily, Jonah washed and dressed, packed his bag and got on board a ship at Joppa. He sighed a long sigh of relief. All the worry and physical exercise had quite tired him out, so he found a corner and fell fast asleep. Soon he began to snore loudly, sounding like a cross between a pig and a whistling kettle.

It wasn't long before a very violent storm blew up. The little boat was tossed about as the waves swept over the top of the mast.

Everyone was very frightened—that is, everyone except Jonah. He was still asleep. The captain shook him violently.

'What now?' Jonah shouted, not at all amused.

'We're going to sink, and all you can do is sleep and snore very loudly!' the captain replied in an equally loud voice. 'You'd better start praying to your god.' As the captain rushed off, Jonah got on to his knees and began to pray.

In the meantime, believing that the storm was a punishment from the gods for something, the sailors had decided to toss a coin in order to find out who was to blame. Guess who it was? Jonah!

'Hey, you!' they shouted to Jonah. 'What have you been up to? Your god is very cross with you.'

Jonah admitted that he was unsuccessfully trying to run away from God.

'You must throw me overboard,' he cried, over the noise of the storm. 'Then everything will be OK!'

Jonah sounded very brave, but inside he was hoping that the crew wouldn't take him up on his offer.

SPLASH! You've guessed it! The sailors threw Jonah into the sea and, sure enough, the storm calmed immediately. As for our gallant hero, Jonah didn't have to swim for long because he was soon swallowed up by a very big fish that God had sent especially for the occasion.

While in the fish's big smelly stomach, Jonah had an opportunity to think about what he'd done. He realized that God is everywhere and you can't run away from him. God knows everything, he is in control of all creation, he has a plan for everyone's life and he doesn't give up easily.

So after the big fish had spat Jonah out on the beach later on, Jonah was ready to say 'Yes' when God asked him once again to go to Nineveh.

When Jonah arrived at Nineveh, God told him what to say to the people. 'Tell them that in forty days I will destroy Nineveh because of their wickedness.'

To cut a long story short, the people of Nineveh were sorry and changed their ways. God forgave them and Jonah wasn't very pleased, because he felt that God should have done what he said he was going to do.

But God is the God of love, who created all things, including people of all nationalities—and he wants to forgive. What's more, he wants us to forgive others as well!

Reproduced with permission from *Stories to Read Aloud* published by BRF 2004 (1 84101 362 5)

Stories from the New Testament

—————— Matthew's Gospel ——————

22

Doing things God's way

Teacher's information

 Bible reference

The story is based on Matthew 4:1–11.

 Theme

When Jesus is tempted to do wrong, he turns to the Bible for guidance.

Key verses

Jesus answered, 'The Scriptures say: "No one can live only on food. People need every word that God has spoken."' ... Jesus answered, 'The Scriptures also say, "Don't try to test the Lord your God!"' ... Jesus answered, 'Go away Satan! The Scriptures say: "Worship the Lord your God and serve only him."'
MATTHEW 4:4, 7, 10

 Talk about…

Ways in which we are tempted to do wrong.

Aim

Not to give in to temptation.

Jigsaw puzzled

Dear God…
Jesus knows how we feel when the devil tempts us, doesn't he?

 Activitime

Bring some different instruction books, including a map and the Bible. Pass them round for the children to look at.

 Jigsaw piece

This incident takes place as Jesus is preparing to begin his ministry.

Prayback

Heavenly Father,
Thank you that Jesus lived in the world as a human being. He experienced temptation, so he understands what we go through, and he showed us how to deal with it.
Please help us to follow Jesus' example—to look to the teaching of the Bible, so that we are prepared to be strong when the devil tempts us to do the wrong thing, and to have the courage to say 'No!' In Jesus' name. Amen

Testing times

After Jesus had been baptized, he wanted to spend some time with his Father God, in order to prepare for the work God had for him to do. He needed to go somewhere quiet, where people wouldn't keep coming to him, asking him to make chairs, tables, cupboards and things like that.

The little carpentry shop where he had worked with Joseph was always full of people wanting things made, but now it was time for Jesus to move on and serve God in a new way.

At his baptism, God had filled Jesus with the Holy Spirit to help him in his work. The Holy Spirit then led Jesus into the desert.

I know that the desert wouldn't be everyone's choice of a holiday location. The view isn't marvellous, it is very hot and there's not much to drink. But Jesus knew it wasn't going to be a holiday. It was away from the rush and bustle of daily life, which was just what he needed.

As he sat down on a rock, Jesus sensed the peacefulness and presence of God. It was wonderful.

The minutes turned into hours, the hours turned into days and the days turned into weeks… Jesus spent forty days in the desert, praying and asking his Father to prepare him for the important work ahead.

During that time, Jesus didn't eat anything, so, as you can imagine, towards the end he was getting quite hungry. That was when he suddenly became aware of a not-very-nice 'presence' that sent a shiver down his spine.

'I can tell you're hungry,' said a cold, unfriendly voice. 'Wouldn't you like something to eat to take away those hunger pains? Surely, if you're the Son of God, you could turn all these stones into bread, and then you would be able to eat as much as you liked. In fact, you could feed all the hungry people in the world, "just like that". That would make you popular!'

Jesus knew who this not-very-nice 'presence' was. It was the devil. His visit was not unexpected.

'I wondered how long it would take for you to turn up,' Jesus commented. 'Just like a bad penny!'

'But what do you think about my suggestion?' the devil persisted.

'I don't think so!' Jesus replied, with conviction. 'I know that food is important, but the Bible says that people have spiritual needs as well, which can only be satisfied by a close relationship with God. My task is all about making that possible.'

The devil was quiet for a moment, but undeterred. 'Let me take you somewhere,' he growled angrily.

It was quite apparent that the devil was a very moody person—with a face like a wet weekend! Anyway, he took Jesus to the top of the temple. It was very high up, high enough to make anyone feel quite dizzy.

'Look at this drop,' the devil shouted,

Reproduced with permission from *Stories to Read Aloud* published by BRF 2004 (1 84101 362 5)

pointing and laughing. 'What about performing some amazing stunts? That would impress people. You'd get lots of followers then. You could throw yourself off here, for starters. God would send a few hundred angels to rescue you in mid-flight. Wouldn't that be quite spectacular?'

Jesus sighed!

'You never give up, do you?' he responded. 'The scriptures say that it is wrong to put God to the test. If people need wild stunts all the time in order to believe, that's not true faith. Nor is it a good basis for a relationship with God.'

The devil thought quickly. This could be his last chance and he was not to be put off.

'Let's go somewhere else,' he said in a sly and devious manner.

He was determined to catch Jesus out somehow and lead him away from God's will. So he took Jesus to the top of a very high mountain and showed him all the nations around. It was a wonderful view. Jesus could see for miles and miles.

'Look at all this,' the devil chuckled. 'Lovely, isn't it? Especially on a summer's day. If you would only work with me, do things my way… immorality, cruelty, selfishness, repression, lies, deceit… you know the kind of thing! We could rule the world together.'

'Go away, Satan,' Jesus replied victoriously. 'You've lost this battle… and don't forget, scripture says that the right thing to do is to worship and serve only God.'

The devil slunk off, defeated. And God sent some angels to attend to Jesus.

Reproduced with permission from *Stories to Read Aloud* published by BRF 2004 (1 84101 362 5)

23

Our response to God's word

Teacher's information

 Bible reference

The story is based on Matthew 13:1–9 and 18–23.

 Theme

Despite much of the seed failing to grow, there will be a harvest.

 Key verse

'The seeds that fell on good ground are the people who hear and understand the message. They produce as much as a hundred or sixty or thirty times what was planted.'
MATTHEW 13:23

 Talk about…

Different types of growth—for example, growth of plants, animals and people; growing in knowledge or confidence; or growing more like Jesus.

 Aim

To grow and produce the spiritual 'fruit' listed in Galatians 5:22–23.

Jigsaw puzzled

Dear God…
How will people know if I am committed to Jesus?

 Activitime

Plant some cress or bean seeds and watch them grow over the next few days or weeks.

 Jigsaw piece

This is one of several parables that Jesus told about his kingdom. A parable is a story about something quite ordinary, but with a deeper meaning as well, about God and his purposes. The deeper meaning will be found only by those who look for it.

Prayback

Almighty God,
Thank you for all the wonderful parables Jesus told, including the parable of the farmer. Please enable us to be like the good soil and produce fruit, demonstrating love, joy, peace, patience, kindness, goodness, faithfulness, gentleness and self-control in our daily lives. Let those around us always enjoy and benefit from that fruit and, because of it, recognize that we are followers of Jesus. In Jesus' name. Amen

---

One for me, one for the birds!

Once upon a time, there was a farmer who lived in a country where it was very rocky, hilly and hot. It was long before the days of machinery, so everything had to be done with hand tools, or using oxen. Planting crops was very hard work and even the farmer's tough, leathery hands would end up covered in blisters by the end of the day.

'Where will you be today, Jethro, my dear?' the farmer's wife asked him one day, as she flung her arms round his neck to be sure of a goodbye kiss.

'I shall be preparing the ground for planting, in the top field,' he replied, as he tried unsuccessfully to struggle free.

His wife smiled as she gave him a big kiss on the cheek. It sounded a bit like a sink plunger at work. 'Now be careful—it's very dangerous up there,' she told him, still holding on to him.

The farmer was not looking forward to the job in hand, because the top field was the most difficult piece of his land to prepare. It was up on the hillside, with many areas that were mainly solid rock with only a few inches of soil on top. And there were always lots of thorn bushes there. He pecked his wife on the cheek, ready to go to work.

'It's a shame that four-wheel-drive tractors, with sprung seats and quadraphonic music centres, haven't been invented yet,' the farmer laughed, as he looked at his watch... then he realized that watches hadn't been invented, either. So he sighed a big sigh.

'You do let your imagination run away with you,' replied his wife, chuckling. 'I don't know where you get it from.'

The farmer's wife was just about to shut the door behind her husband when she called him back.

'Don't forget to take your goatskin gloves to protect your hands,' she instructed, as she gave them to him.

All day the farmer struggled, ploughing and harrowing with his two oxen. The plough kept catching on rocks and Jethro kept getting his clothes caught up on the thorn bushes. The sweat poured from him, but at last the soil was ready to plant the seed in.

'I'll plant the seed tomorrow, boys,' he said to the oxen as they walked home for tea.

Sure enough, the farmer got up early the next morning and went to the top field to plant the seed. He carried the seed in a large basket and, as he walked up and down the field, he threw the seed on to the land, spreading it as evenly as he could. It was another long day. When he had finished planting, he walked home, carrying his hand tools and the empty seed basket.

Unfortunately, some of the seed had fallen on to the hard, stony pathway, where it lay until the hungry birds came and ate it.

Some of the seed fell where the ground was rocky and the soil wasn't very deep, so it grew up quickly, but soon died because it had hardly any roots.

Quite a lot of seed fell where there were lots of thorn bushes, so as the seed grew there, the thorn bushes choked the young plants.

Thankfully, however, a lot of the seed fell on the good ground that Jethro had prepared.

And it produced a lovely crop for him and his family.

'All I need now is a combine harvester,' the farmer laughed to himself—letting his imagination run away with him yet again!

Perhaps this is just a story about growing some seed—nothing more. If the seed is planted and tended in the right way, it will grow and produce a bumper harvest. It's nice to know that our farmers have that assurance! So that's it…

There again, perhaps not! What if we were the soil, and the seed was the message of Jesus? In that case, Jesus is saying that when we are truly committed to him—praying, studying the Bible, worshipping, and serving him—then people will see the evidence of that commitment by the fruit that we produce.

I expect, when that old farmer harvested his crops, lots of people benefited from the fruit of the harvest. So will those around us when we produce spiritual fruit—love, joy, peace, patience, kindness, goodness, faithfulness, gentleness and self-control.

Reproduced with permission from *Stories to Read Aloud* published by BRF 2004 (1 84101 362 5)

24

Jesus can do wonderful things with our lives

Teacher's information

 Bible reference

The story is based on Matthew 14:13–21.

 Theme

With things as small and insignificant as two tiny fish and five bread rolls, Jesus satisfies the hunger of the vast crowd.

 Key verses

Jesus asked his disciples to bring the food to him, and he told the crowd to sit down on the grass. Jesus took the five loaves and two fish. He looked up towards heaven and blessed the food. Then he broke the bread and handed it to his disciples, and they gave it to the people. After everyone had eaten all they wanted, Jesus' disciples picked up twelve large baskets of leftovers.
MATTHEW 14:18–20

 Talk about...

How we can help to make the world a better place.

 Aim

To give our lives to Jesus, to be used by him, to do his work on earth.

Jigsaw puzzled

Dear God…
Can I really help you do your work?

 Activitime

See if you can share one small packed lunch among the whole group. It doesn't go far, does it? **NB:** To ensure safety, make sure you know beforehand of any food allergies that the children might have.

 Jigsaw piece

This is one of the most well-known miracles of Jesus. It happens just after the death of his cousin, John the Baptist.

Prayback

God of miracles,
We thank you for this wonderful miracle—that Jesus was able to use very ordinary and insignificant things to make a tremendous difference to a large number of people. Please use our lives in this way, and help us to make the world a better place.
Show us the people whose lives you want to touch, through us. We do pray for people who are hungry, as well, that they will have food to eat. In Jesus' name. Amen

Did anyone bring the hamper?

Jesus had gone for a boat trip to get away from it all. He'd just heard that his cousin, John the Baptist, had been killed, so obviously he was upset and needed a bit of time on his own. Having said that, Jesus didn't have much 'quiet time', because when the boat landed on the shore, a large crowd was waiting for him.

'Shall we tell them to go away?' his friends asked, very concerned about Jesus.

But Jesus felt sorry for the people, who had walked miles to see him. Their needs were so great.

'Don't worry,' he said to his friends, smiling. 'That boat trip was quite a long break for me. Besides, there's work to do.'

There were so many people at the shore who needed his help. They had been brought by families and friends to see him. They had all manner of things wrong with them—from warts and ingrown toenails to life-threatening diseases.

'I want to see!' came a voice.

'I want to walk again!' came another.

'Make my mummy better!' a little child shouted out.

'Can you change the shape of my nose?' a rather vain middle-aged lady shouted. 'I've never liked it this way! It looks more like a carrot.'

Jesus hardly knew where to start.

'One at a time,' he said in a kind but firm voice. 'Don't push, please—there's plenty of time.'

You know what it's like when you're busy— time just slips by. Well, it certainly did on that occasion. The sun began to set. In the background, people began murmuring.

'I keep thinking about food,' grumbled one person.

'My stomach thinks that my throat has been cut,' groaned someone else.

'I'm so hungry, I could eat a donkey,' a little boy shouted out, looking round to see if anyone had arrived on one.

Jesus' friends reached breaking point when a rather large gentleman suggested, quite forcibly, that they ought to be doing something about the situation.

Reproduced with permission from *Stories to Read Aloud* published by BRF 2004 (1 84101 362 5)

'The crowd are getting hungry,' they told Jesus. 'We need to send everyone away to buy food.'

'No need,' Jesus laughed confidently. 'You feed them!'

The men were stunned into silence for a moment. Then they began to argue about who should organize things. It turned out that, between them, they had nothing to eat, and there were no burger bars or takeaways in those days.

'I know,' exclaimed one of the men. 'Let's ask the crowd what food they've brought with them.'

They did just that, but most of the people had already eaten what they had brought, a long time ago. So when it came to the pooling of resources, they only had two small fish and five bread rolls.

'I eat that much myself for my mid-morning snack,' said one of Jesus' friends, inspecting the tiny picnic.

'Last one to the front of the crowd has to explain to Jesus that this is all the food we've got,' one of the more athletic men cried out, as he began to run. It was a bit embarrassing, taking such a small offering to Jesus.

When Jesus sat everyone down for a 'meal', the men cringed.

'There must be more than five thousand people,' one of them observed. 'It will be a slimmer's diet today!'

But, to everyone's surprise, as Jesus broke the bread and gave thanks for it, it seemed to just keep coming. It was quite amazing! The same thing happened with the fish. Everyone had more than enough to eat, and there was more left over at the end than there had been to start with.

I think we can safely say that this miracle demonstrated Jesus' power to take something very small and insignificant and do a very wonderful thing with it. And what he can do with bread and fish, he can do with our lives. Sounds good to me!

Reproduced with permission from *Stories to Read Aloud* published by BRF 2004 (1 84101 362 5)

25

Stepping out in faith

Teacher's information

 Bible reference

The story is based on Matthew 14:22–33.

 Theme

When Jesus calls Peter, Peter steps out of the boat believing that Jesus will enable him to walk on the water. And, for a few steps, Peter does it!

 Key verse

'Come on!' Jesus said. Peter then got out of the boat and started walking on the water towards him.
MATTHEW 14:29

 Talk about…

What a 'step of faith' is.

 Aim

To believe that God can do the things that he says he will, and act upon it.

Jigsaw puzzled

Dear God…
What happens when I step out in faith?

 Activitime

Arrange for someone to perform a conjuring trick. But remember, it's just an illusion.

 Jigsaw piece

This story is not an illusion. It is one of Jesus' many miracles. He and Peter do the impossible.

Prayback

Gracious God,
Thank you that whatever you ask us to do, you equip us for it, and you are the God who can do the impossible. Please help us to be prepared to step out in confidence and do the things you would have us do, knowing that you will be with us in those situations. In Jesus' name. Amen

I'm with you, Jesus!

'I feel a lot better now I've had something to eat,' commented one of Jesus' friends as he grinned contentedly.

The others were more interested in where the meal had come from. It's not every day that more than five thousand people are fed with only five bread rolls and two small fish.

'If I hadn't seen it with my own two eyes, I wouldn't have believed it,' another said in amazement.

'And we've got enough food left over for a snack later,' responded one of the heavier lads, licking his lips.

Jesus smiled as he listened to his friends chatting together. Then he coughed to get their attention.

'I need to go somewhere quiet to pray, after I have sent the crowd home,' he told them. 'You go on ahead, across the lake in the boat, and I'll meet up with you later.'

It was dark when the men climbed into the small fishing boat and pushed away from the shore.

'It's a little bit spooky,' one of them commented nervously. 'It's enough to give you goose bumps.'

'Whoooo! Whoooooo!' another said, in fun.

'Who believes in ghosts, then?' a third asked.

There were mixed views, but the discussion left them feeling more than a little jumpy.

'Let's just concentrate on rowing,' it was suggested. They agreed that ghosts were nonsense.

At first, it was easy to row, but then the wind got up and the waves beat against the boat. Soon they were struggling to keep going.

By this time, Jesus had finished praying and was ready to catch them up. He decided to demonstrate God's power, once again, by walking across the lake on the water.

You can imagine the situation. It was only just beginning to get light, so visibility was bad. The water was rough, and the men were anxious about the weather. Of course, when one of them spotted a shadowy figure walking across the lake, it was the last straw.

'Ahhhhh!'

'Help!'

'It's a ghost coming to get us!'

Everyone was terrified—until they heard a voice that they knew.

'It's only me, lads. There's no need to panic. You can stop shaking now.'

It was Jesus!

As most of the group were heaving a sigh of relief, suddenly, to everyone's surprise, Peter shouted out, 'Wait for me, Lord. I'm coming out to you. Just give me the word, and I'll step over the edge of the boat.'

'You crazy old fool, Peter. You'll sink,' all the others teased him.

'You watch me,' Peter said, with courage and determination. 'I'll show you!'

Jesus smiled at Peter. 'Come on, then. I'm waiting for you.'

Believing that Jesus had the power to enable him to walk on the water, Peter jumped out of the boat, in faith. One step, two steps… He turned to the others.

'Look at me,' he shouted triumphantly. 'I'm walking on the water!'

Suddenly, he realized that what he was doing was impossible, totally panicked and began to sink.

'Help me! I'm drowning!' he yelled.

But it was all right, because Jesus reached out and grabbed hold of Peter. Moments later, Jesus and Peter were safely in the little boat, greeted by open mouths.

As Jesus sat down, his friends turned to him and, feeling very humbled, exclaimed, 'You really are God's Son, aren't you?'

Jesus didn't say anything. He just glanced over at Peter, who was a bit shaken up, and smiled warmly. He had great hopes for Peter. Peter didn't achieve everything he set out to, but he was always ready to have a go and 'step out in faith'—and that's important!

26

Salvation is a gift

 Bible reference

The story is based on Matthew 19:16–26.

 Theme

Salvation is a gift, which the young man will receive if he follows Jesus. It cannot be bought.

 Key verse

Jesus replied, 'If you want to be perfect, go and sell everything you own! Give the money to the poor, and you will have riches in heaven. Then come and be my follower.'
MATTHEW 19:21

 Talk about...

Things that we can't buy.

 Aim

To understand that money and possessions only have value in this life, and that value is limited.

Jigsaw puzzled

Dear God...
Can free things really be more valuable than the things that we save up for and buy, or earn?

 Activitime

Cut out adverts from newspapers or magazines offering free gifts. Are they really free?

 Jigsaw piece

During Jesus' ministry, he was often asked questions—sometimes trick ones to trap him. This particular question, however, is a genuine one.

Prayback

God who loves to give good gifts,
Thank you that we don't have to earn our way into a close friendship with you or into heaven. Thank you that your forgiveness is free when we follow Jesus. Thank you that, through following him, we are brought into a close relationship with you and are assured of a home in heaven, for ever, surrounded by all your wonderful blessings. Please help each one of us to accept that free gift. In Jesus' name. Amen

You can't buy eternal life

One of my favourite stories in the Bible involves a young man who asked a very good question. Jesus had been busy teaching and blessing children. He was just about to move on when the young man ran up to him, out of breath.

'Teacher, you're a good person. What good thing must I do to live for ever?' he asked, as he struggled to get his breath back.

He wasn't looking for the secret of not growing old. He was asking what he had to do to make his life right with God, and be assured of a place in heaven. People today would probably just say, 'What must I do to become a Christian?' or some people might talk about receiving 'eternal life'.

I expect the young man probably went to the synagogue regularly (that's the Jewish church) and tried to follow the law of God to some extent. But he still felt that something was missing. Anyway, Jesus stopped to talk to him.

'You can't earn your way to heaven by doing good deeds, you know,' he said sympathetically but firmly. 'It's not like paying in to a pension scheme. No one could possibly live a life good enough to earn their way to heaven.'

But the young man still didn't seem to be convinced.

'Think about it,' Jesus said kindly. 'What does the law of God say?'

The young man smiled. He knew the answer to this question, because he'd learned it all off by heart as a child.

'Do not murder anyone, do not be unfaithful to your marriage partner, do not steal, do not tell lies about anyone, do not cheat, respect your mum and dad... I've kept these since I was a small lad,' he answered excitedly. 'You can't catch me out,' he challenged—rather full of himself.

Jesus sighed a deep sigh of compassionate despair. The young man reminded him of a child who had been spoiled.

'What am I going to do with you?' Jesus whispered to him, wanting to help him to understand. 'I'm just going to have to spell it out to you, aren't I?'

Reproduced with permission from *Stories to Read Aloud* published by BRF 2004 (1 84101 362 5)

Jesus had hoped that when he'd asked the young man about the law, he would have realized for himself that he had failed to keep it—many times. He hadn't been good, because apart from God the Father, Jesus and the Holy Spirit, no one is really good! He had never put God first because he'd always put money first in his life, and the things that it could buy.

'What I'm going to say to you now will come very hard,' Jesus told the young man. 'The thing you need to do is to sell all that you have, use the money responsibly to help others, and follow me—trust me, follow my example, do the things that I tell you to do. Then you will be forgiven, and you will have what you asked for in your question.'

The young man's head was spinning. He'd never realized that he wasn't living according to God's law. He had certainly never realized that going to heaven was something that couldn't be earned, but was a free gift—a gift given to those who followed Jesus and were genuinely sorry for the wrong things that they had done.

He thought about his large house, his camels, his jewels, his gold, his silver… He jangled his pocket full of coins and smiled. He remembered the expensive holiday that he had just booked.

'I can't take all of this in,' the young man gasped as he turned and left.

He felt strange as he crept away from Jesus. Despite all his wealth, he felt empty inside. It felt as if he had lost his best friend and would never see him again.

I like to think that maybe the young man went back later, having changed his mind— but we're not told that in the Bible.

But you know, even now, many people still try to earn their way into God's favour. Jesus 'paid the price' when he died on the cross. Why is it that some people just can't accept a gift, when it is offered to them on a plate?

27

Building God's kingdom

Teacher's information

 Bible reference

The story is based on Matthew 21:1–17.

 Theme

God's kingdom is anywhere that Jesus reigns as king.

 Key verse

Announce to the people of Jerusalem: 'Your king is coming to you! He is humble and rides on a donkey. He comes on the colt of a donkey.' MATTHEW 21:5

 Talk about…

Ways in which we can influence people by what we say and do.

 Aim

To make our homes, schools, workplaces and church fellowships into God's kingdom, by living according to his will in those situations—making Jesus king.

Jigsaw puzzled

Dear God…
When is your kingdom coming?

 Activitime

Write your name at the top of a sheet of paper and list underneath all the groups that you belong to. They are places and situations where your behaviour can influence others—for example, when you're with your family, at church, in school or involved with clubs.

 Jigsaw piece

This story marks the completion of Jesus' journey to Jerusalem, for what is known as the 'last supper'. As a result of this journey, after a series of events, Jesus is crucified.

Prayback

Lord Jesus, King of kings,
Thank you that, by living our lives according to your ways, we can make the places where we live, work and play into your kingdom. Please enable us to do that. Through your power, let your kingdom grow and spread. Amen

Quite a visit!

Jesus and his friends were continuing their journey to Jerusalem, and they were nearing Bethphage on the Mount of Olives. Suddenly, Jesus turned to two of his friends.

'What do you two know about donkeys?' he asked them.

'They've got four legs, they bite, they kick, and are rather awkward,' one of them replied.

'He's just kidding,' the other one said, laughing. 'Why do you want to know?'

It turned out that Jesus wanted a young donkey colt for the day—to ride into Jerusalem. He told the two men just where to find one.

'He's not used to being away from his mother, so you'd better bring her along as well,' Jesus told them. 'And he's never been ridden before.'

The group looked at Jesus to see if he was serious. Sure enough, he wasn't joking.

'Is that wise?' one of the men asked, after a moment.

'Everything is according to God's plan,' Jesus replied confidently. 'It is all predicted in scripture.'

As the two men went to find the donkeys, they began to argue about who would lead the colt. Well, to put it more accurately, they were both coming up with excuses for not leading him.

'I'm allergic to donkey hair,' one of them moaned, as he pretended to sneeze very loudly.

'I've got a bad back,' the other whinged. 'If I strain it, I'll be in bed for a week!'

Anyway, eventually they found the donkeys, had a word with the owner and both men rather fell in love with the colt—so everything was all right.

After putting a coat across the colt's back, Jesus climbed on and began to ride the last bit of their journey. The colt behaved very well, even when he saw the vast crowd of people waiting for them when they arrived at Jerusalem.

What a welcome that was! The crowds threw coats and branches all over the road, to form a carpet for Jesus to ride over. They

Reproduced with permission from *Stories to Read Aloud* published by BRF 2004 (1 84101 362 5)

waved their arms excitedly and shouted their praises out as Jesus rode by.

It was a very joyful and uplifting occasion and, as Jesus had told his friends, a fulfilment of Old Testament prophecy. It was like a cross between a carnival procession and a royal visit—but with a humble simplicity about it.

Jesus' friends were full of excitement. They really thought the kingdom that Jesus talked about so much had come at last.

But then, minutes later, Jesus was in the temple, turning over the money changers' tables and driving out the salesmen. It was chaos—people pushing and shoving, trying to catch the pigeons that had escaped, others picking up the money… a free-for-all.

'This is not what the temple is for. It should be a place of prayer,' Jesus said firmly.

'That's not going to make him very popular with the priests and Pharisees,' the lads whispered to each other.

When Jesus' friends looked again, Jesus was healing people who were unwell, and the children were running around, still shouting praises to him. The priests and Pharisees didn't like that, either. Trouble was brewing! You can be sure that wherever Jesus was, there would be someone hiding in the shadows who didn't approve.

It must be said that Palm Sunday was a mixed sort of a day. It started off with the followers of Jesus praising and worshipping him as if he was a king, with great joy and excitement. Later on, Jesus made a judgment against evil in the temple. Then he moved on to healing people who came to him. And the day finished with the priests and Pharisees plotting against Jesus.

Could this be a glimpse of how the kingdom will be overshadowed by the sinful world we live in, until Jesus' return? I think so!

Reproduced with permission from *Stories to Read Aloud* published by BRF 2004 (1 84101 362 5)

28

Heaven

Teacher's information

 Bible reference

The story is based on Matthew 22:1–14.

 Theme

Jesus compares heaven to a wedding banquet. It is full of good things, including the love and presence of God. But not everyone will be allowed in.

 Key verses

When the king went in to meet the guests, he found that one of them wasn't wearing the right kind of clothes for the wedding. The king asked, 'Friend, why didn't you wear proper clothes for the wedding?' But the guest had no excuse. So the king gave orders for that person to be tied hand and foot and to be thrown outside into the dark. That's where people will cry and grit their teeth in pain.
MATTHEW 22:11–13

 Talk about…

Going to a wedding.

 Aim

To accept our invitation to heaven, and to receive Jesus' forgiveness.

> **Jigsaw puzzled**
>
> *Dear God…*
> *Does everyone go to heaven?*

 Activitime

Design a wedding invitation card, leaving spaces for the name of the person who is doing the inviting and the name of the person who is being invited. In the first space write 'Jesus', and in the second write your own name, so that Jesus is inviting you.

 Jigsaw piece

This is one of Jesus' parables. It is all about heaven. An interesting point is that one person is not allowed to join the feast!

> **Prayback**
>
> *Lord Jesus,*
> *Thank you that you died on the cross, so that, through following you, we can be forgiven for the wrong things that we have done and know that one day we will have a home in heaven. Please help us, and others, not to make excuses when faced with that decision. Amen*

Everything is provided

I suppose if Jesus was telling this story today, it might be slightly different—not in its content, but in the way it was told. No doubt he would bring modern technology into it. Maybe it would go something like this…

Heaven is a bit like a king throwing a wedding feast for his son. What a privilege it would be for the guests to be invited into the presence of the royal family. It would be a time of joy and celebration, bringing together people who loved each other and giving an opportunity to enjoy a banquet of good things.

'There's not long to go now,' the king said to his private secretary, excitedly. He handed him a very long list.

'We need to get the invitations sorted out quickly. Here are the names of everyone who we want to come.'

The secretary scurried off to his PC to prepare the wording and artwork for the task. After that, he got busy sending e-mails, until everyone had been notified of the occasion.

Time went by. Everything was arranged—the venue, the food, the music, the officials and helpers. Even wedding clothes were provided for the use of the guests. There were some lovely dresses for the ladies, and big floppy hats like huge fancy dustbin lids!

'Everything is ready!' the king shouted, tired but happy.

It was such a relief. The king felt that a great weight had been taken off his shoulders. He turned to his private secretary once again.

'Send out some more e-mails as reminders to the invited guests. Tell them that everything is ready, so RSVP. Anyone you can't get in touch with easily, go and tell them personally.'

And so it was done.

To the king's shock and horror, when the replies came, they were not what he wanted to hear. Instead of people accepting the invitation, recognizing it as the privilege that it was, excuses came flooding in.

'I've just bought the most wonderful villa in Florida—four bedrooms (each with en-suite bathroom), the most amazing kitchen, a huge lounge, a separate dining-room and a

Reproduced with permission from *Stories to Read Aloud* published by BRF 2004 (1 84101 362 5)

swimming pool. You know what it's like—I have to go and try it out. Sorry, can't come to the wedding!'

'You know, I've been so looking forward to coming to the wedding. But business is business. I have to follow up a huge contract. We could be talking millions of pounds here. Another time, perhaps…'

And some just shut the door in the face of the servant who took out the personal invitations.

The king was not pleased. So, after dealing with those who had abused his offer, he threw the wedding party open to anyone who wished to come. People came from all over the world for the wonderful occasion. The celebrations began. It was the kind of wedding feast that everyone had dreamed about—a bit like a fairytale.

However, after a little while, there was a bit of a commotion. A man was being thrown out because he hadn't bothered to wear the wedding clothes that had been provided. What a terrible shame that he had got so close, but was turned out because he thought he could come to the wedding without using the suit that had been provided. It was a lovely suit as well, and the right size!

And so it will be with heaven. It's going to be wonderful—a place of joy, celebration, love, peace and healing, where God the Father, Jesus and the Holy Spirit will be present. Everyone has been invited. To accept, all we have to do is follow Jesus…

But many will not accept the invitation. Not everyone will accept the forgiveness that Jesus offers for the wrong things that they have done, which is the only way that we can get in. You've got it—the wedding clothes represent that forgiveness!

Reproduced with permission from *Stories to Read Aloud* published by BRF 2004 (1 84101 362 5)

Using all that we have and are for Jesus

Teacher's information

 ### Bible reference

The story is based on Matthew 26:6–13.

 ### Theme

The woman gives what is probably her most treasured possession to Jesus.

 ### Key verse

A woman came in with a bottle of expensive perfume and poured it on Jesus' head.
MATTHEW 26:7

 ### Talk about...

Possessions that we value, and why we value them.

 ### Aim

To use our possessions, our time, and the things that we can do, wisely and generously for Jesus.

Jigsaw puzzled

Dear God...
Must I share my possessions and use my abilities for others?

 ### Activitime

Make a list of things that you are good at doing.

 ### Jigsaw piece

This event happens just before Jesus and his disciples celebrate the Passover feast in Jerusalem (known as the 'last supper'). It will not be long before Jesus is crucified.

Prayback

Generous heavenly Father,
    Thank you for all the good gifts that you give to us—for our homes that we live in, the cars that we travel in, clothes that keep us warm, and all the other things that make us comfortable and bring us enjoyment and satisfaction. Thank you for all the abilities and the time that you have given to each one of us. Please help us to use all these things wisely and generously, for the work of Jesus. In Jesus' name. Amen

That smells nice!

I'm going to tell you a story about a woman who, quite unintentionally, became very famous for doing something unusual. The only trouble is that we aren't told her name, so we can't be quite sure who she was. It happened at a difficult time for Jesus, because he knew that soon he was going to be crucified. He kept trying to tell his friends, but they didn't seem to understand.

One day, Jesus was enjoying his dinner—a good friend of his, called Simon, had asked him round to his home.

'We're going to have a bit of a party—a few friends, the latest harp music—you know! Will you come?' Simon had asked.

Jesus had enquired if he could bring his friends with him.

'The more, the merrier,' Simon had laughed. 'Bring a wineskin!'

Anyway, having all arrived at Simon's house in good time for the party, they were in the middle of dinner when it happened. There was a lot of talking and laughter. Jesus' friends were telling the latest stories about the miracles that they had seen him perform.

Then suddenly, just as they were about to start pudding, a woman rushed up to Jesus. To everyone's surprise, she started pouring some expensive and very sweet-smelling perfume on to Jesus' head. When I say expensive, I mean E-X-P-E-N-S-I-V-E! The room smelt like a cottage garden full of roses.

It wasn't long before Jesus' friends started moaning.

'What a waste.'

'It could have been sold.'

'Just think what we could have done with all that money.'

'Was this woman invited to the party, anyway?'

Then Jesus held up his hands to catch their attention.

'Hey! Stop that!' he said, gently reprimanding them. 'This woman has given me this wonderful perfume as a demonstration of her love for me. I shall soon be killed, and she has anointed my body for burial.'

The lads looked blankly at Jesus, still not understanding what he was talking about.

The woman who interrupted the party had given Jesus probably her most valuable possession. She seems to have wanted to give all that she had and was to Jesus. And at the same time, she seems to have been one of the few people who understood that Jesus was going to be killed very soon.

It's easy to criticize. But, in doing so, the other people at the party missed seeing these reasons behind the woman's generosity. What is our attitude to the treasured possessions, time and abilities that we have? Are we prepared to give them to Jesus?

Well, then Jesus turned round to his friends and smiled.

'This young woman is going to be famous for what she has just done,' he told them. 'People all over the world, for years to come, will tell this story.'

Speaking 2000 years later, I think he could have been right!

Reproduced with permission from *Stories to Read Aloud* published by BRF 2004 (1 84101 362 5)

30

What Jesus has done for us

Teacher's information

 Bible reference

The story is based on Matthew 26:17–35 and 1 Corinthians 11:23–26.

 Theme

Jesus tells his disciples that his death will enable people to be forgiven for the wrong things that they have done.

 Key verses

During the meal Jesus took some bread in his hands. He blessed the bread and broke it. Then he gave it to his disciples and said, 'Take this and eat it. This is my body.' Jesus picked up a cup of wine and gave thanks to God. He then gave it to his disciples and said, 'Take this and drink it. This is my blood, and with it God makes his agreement with you. It will be poured out, so that many people will have their sins forgiven.'
MATTHEW 26:26–28

 Talk about…

Things that we do wrong.

 Aim

To understand why Jesus had to die on the cross.

Jigsaw puzzled

Dear God…
Did Jesus die on the cross for me?

 Activitime

Bring a glass of wine and some bread or wafers. Explain that the bread and wine are used in the Communion service, but not everyone understands why.

 Jigsaw piece

Towards the end of Jesus' ministry on earth, he meets with his friends for a meal. He knows that he will soon die, after being betrayed by one of his friends. But he also has something very important to tell them about why he has to die.

Prayback

Loving Lord Jesus,
Thank you that you died on the cross for everyone, paying the penalty for the wrong things that we have done—but you are alive today! Thank you that when we say 'sorry' and turn to you, we receive your forgiveness. Please help us never to forget what you have done for us. Amen

A special meal

It was nearly Passover—the time when people remembered God saving the Israelites from death during the last of the ten plagues in Egypt.

'Where are we going to eat the Passover feast this year?' Jesus' friends asked excitedly.

Jesus had got it all arranged. He told them where to go and what to do. His friends went off up the road, chatting together, to get things ready.

'I'm not doing the washing-up this year,' one of them said defiantly. 'It makes my hands go all wrinkly, just like prunes.'

'I did it last year,' another responded.

'Come on, guys, we haven't even got the meal ready yet, and you're arguing about who's washing up,' a third said, in an attempt to keep the peace.

Anyway, once they had found the place where they were going to celebrate the Passover, some of them started to set the table. Meanwhile, others headed up the road to do some shopping. This would not have involved an uncontrollable trolley in the supermarket, or a 'buy two, get one free' offer. I expect it would have been a visit to a few busy little market stalls.

'Don't forget the bread,' one of the disciples shouted after those who were heading towards the market.

'And the wine,' someone else called out.

'It's all right, we've got a list,' came the reply, just before the shoppers disappeared round the corner.

At last, everything was ready and Jesus arrived. His friends were laughing and chattering together.

'Let's eat now,' Jesus announced, smiling kindly. 'I'm sure you're all hungry.'

However, after a short while, Jesus stopped eating. After finishing his mouthful, he began to speak.

'There is something I have to tell you,' he said firmly but with a note of sadness in his voice. 'One of you is going to betray me.'

Suddenly, his friends lost their appetites. They all denied being 'the one'.

'I would never do such a thing,' Judas said, with insincerity in his voice.

Reproduced with permission from *Stories to Read Aloud* published by BRF 2004 (1 84101 362 5)

'Yes, you would,' Jesus replied, 'because you are the one!'

The whole room went silent for what seemed like minutes, but it was probably only seconds.

Jesus picked up a loaf of bread, gave thanks to God and, breaking it into pieces, handed it round the table.

'Eat this,' he told his friends. 'This bread is like my body. Soon it will be broken for you all and I will go through terrible pain.'

Then Jesus took the cup of wine, gave thanks to God for it and handed it round.

'Drink some of this wine, all of you,' he continued. 'This wine is like my blood being poured out for you. I am going to die very soon so that everyone will have the opportunity to be forgiven and set free from all the consequences of the things they have done wrong.'

After the meal, Jesus and his friends sang a hymn together. Then they all went up to the Mount of Olives—all except Judas, that is. As they walked, Jesus talked about what was to happen very soon.

'Tonight you will all desert me,' he said sadly. 'But I'll see you all again when I've risen.'

Of course, everyone denied that they would desert Jesus, but he smiled and quietly replied that they would.

Jesus' friends didn't realize what he had been trying to tell them, until quite a lot later. Jesus had been warning them that he would die a terrible death on the cross, paying the penalty for all the wrong things that were ever done—past, present and future. As a result, we would all have the opportunity to be forgiven for all the things that we have ever done wrong—by saying 'sorry' and trying to live the way Jesus would want us to.

One more thing—after the feast, Jesus said something very important. He told us to continue to share bread and wine together, so that we would never forget what he has done for us.

Reproduced with permission from *Stories to Read Aloud* published by BRF 2004 (1 84101 362 5)

Stories from the New Testament

—————— Mark's Gospel ——————

31

God's power over evil

Teacher's information

 Bible reference

The story is based on Mark 5:1–20.

 Theme

The people can see God's power over evil at work in Jesus, because they know what the man in the story used to be like.

 Key verse

When they came to Jesus, they saw the man who had once been full of demons. He was sitting there with his clothes on and in his right mind, and they were terrified.

MARK 5:15

 Talk about…

Ways in which evil is evident in the world today.

 Aim

To realize that the only hope for the world to become a better place is through the power of God.

Jigsaw puzzled

Dear God…
Is the evil in the world out of control?

 Activitime

Think up an imaginary title for a newspaper in New Testament times, and write it in large fancy letters at the top of a sheet of paper. After hearing the story, write a headline that describes it and give a brief account of what happened. Do it in the style of a newspaper article.

 Jigsaw piece

This incident takes place on the eastern side of the Sea of Galilee—a mainly non-Jewish, or 'Gentile', area, hence the large herd of pigs. It was while Jesus and his friends were crossing the lake to come here that Jesus calmed the storm.

Prayback

Almighty God,
We thank you that you are more powerful even than the devil, and that, through Jesus, you have won the victory over evil—even though the battle is not yet over. Please protect us from the effects of evil in the world today. Help us not to be tempted to do the work of the devil, and, through your power, make the world a better place. In Jesus' name. Amen

Now who's strange?

'Well, that was some crossing!' exclaimed one of Jesus' friends, still a little shaky. 'It's not every day that you see someone calm a storm just by talking to it,' another responded, still in a daze.

As Jesus and his friends approached the shore in the little fishing boat, they saw a very strange-looking man watching them from a distance. His hair and beard were very long and tatty, all his clothes were torn, his body was covered in cuts and grazes, he was very dirty and he was behaving very oddly.

'Oh no! Look who's waiting for us,' one of the men groaned. 'I wonder what he wants.'

'I wonder what he smells like,' another commented.

'We'll soon find out.'

The man was jumping up and down rather menacingly, a bit like a large silverback gorilla. Everyone began to argue about who would have to get out of the boat first to meet this weird person. But as they reached the shore,

Jesus jumped out before anyone else.

As soon as Jesus' feet touched dry land, the strange man ran towards him, shouting and waving his arms with a kind of flapping motion. He looked more like an angry bird of prey now.

'Watch out!' Jesus' friends all shouted together, getting ready to make a quick getaway. (Having said that, they didn't particularly want to get back into the boat again.)

When the man reached Jesus, he fell on to his knees in front of him, shouting at the top of his voice. Jesus looked at his poor distorted face, full of pain and anguish, and felt compassion for him.

'Come out, evil spirit!' Jesus commanded.

'Why have you come after me? What do you want?' the man responded.

This unfortunate person had got quite a reputation for hanging around tombs and being generally violent and uncontrollable.

'What's your name?' Jesus asked him.

He replied that his name was Legion, because there were many evil spirits in him.

Recognizing Jesus' power, the evil spirits begged him to let them go into a herd of pigs

Reproduced with permission from *Stories to Read Aloud* published by BRF 2004 (1 84101 362 5)

that were rooting around in a nearby field. The pigs looked so contented, with their mud-covered snouts and little curly tails, but Jesus gave the evil spirits permission. As they entered the pigs, the animals seemed to go mad and rushed down a very steep bank into the lake, where they all drowned.

'Hey, what have you done to my pigs?' the man who was in charge of them shouted, as he leapt up and down in anger.

'I'm going to tell my boss of you!' he yelled, running off towards the nearby town.

Word about the unusual event spread quickly, but by the time people came to see for themselves, the strange man was no longer strange. He'd had a bath and a haircut, put some clean clothes on and was sitting quietly, listening to Jesus.

The whole event frightened the people of that area so much that they wanted Jesus and his disciples to leave as soon as possible—if not sooner!

'Can I come with you and help you?' the man asked Jesus, as they walked over to the boat.

'You can do more good by going home and telling your family and friends what God has done for you,' Jesus replied, smiling. 'They'll be able to see for themselves that it's true.'

With that, Jesus and his friends climbed into the boat and pushed away from the shore. They waved to the man whose life had been transformed—another successful mission. God is more powerful than any evil spirit and than the devil himself.

Reproduced with permission from *Stories to Read Aloud* published by BRF 2004 (1 84101 362 5)

32

Jesus the healer

Teacher's information

 Bible reference

The story is taken from Mark 5:21–34.

 Theme

The woman knows that if she reaches out and touches Jesus, she will be healed from her illness.

 Key verse

She had said to herself, 'If I can just touch his clothes, I will get well.'
MARK 5:28

 Talk about...

Things that people need healing for—physical illness, mental illness, stress, anxiety, sadness, loneliness, fear, guilt and so on.

 Aim

That we will reach out to Jesus for help when we feel frightened, lonely or worried.

Jigsaw puzzled

Dear God...
What should I do when I'm frightened?

 Activitime

Draw an outline of a hand on a sheet of paper, using your own hand to draw round. After the story, in each of the fingers and the thumb write down a time when you might need to receive Jesus' healing touch—for example, when you are worried.

 Jigsaw piece

During Jesus' ministry, he was continually being asked to heal people. The healing in this story takes place while someone else is speaking to Jesus about healing his daughter.

Prayback

Heavenly Father,
Thank you that when we pray to you in the name of Jesus, however many other people are praying to you at the same time, you still hear our individual prayers. We thank you that Jesus healed the woman in the story and he still heals people today. Please help us with the things for which we need healing. In Jesus' name. Amen

Just a touch

Doris knew all about queuing up at the surgery, waiting for appointment after appointment with her doctor, and hearing the same old words: 'What seems to be the trouble today, Mrs Wigglesworth?'

She never knew what to say in reply. She felt bad, going back time and time again for the same thing.

'Oh, it's the usual,' she'd eventually say, with a nervous smile.

Then it would be off to the hospital again for scans, miniature cameras performing investigations, blood tests—the lot! But their efforts were always unsuccessful.

'We can't find anything that could be causing your symptoms,' Doris would be told once again.

Well, that's how the story might have gone if it had happened recently. But the woman in today's story lived in New Testament times, before modern technology and before the National Health Service and health insurance.

We don't know what her name was, so let's still call her Doris.

Doris had suffered with some kind of internal bleeding for twelve years. She'd been right through the health system of the time, and it had taken all her money in return. She had been left penniless, but just as ill as ever.

'What am I going to do?' she asked herself out loud one day, in total despair. Doris felt as if she was in a deep, dark hole and there was no way out.

Then she remembered a friend telling her about a wonderful man who was in the area, who performed miracles. He'd made the blind see, and paralysed people walk… maybe he could help her.

Doris put on her best coat—well, actually, it was her only coat—and she went to find Jesus. When she eventually spotted him, she couldn't believe the size of the crowd round him. It looked like people queuing for an important football match.

Doris climbed up on to a large rock that lay on the ground and peered over the tops of people's heads. A wealthy man was talking to Jesus. He was asking Jesus to heal his dying daughter.

'The healer's not going to want to speak to me,' Doris muttered, 'not when he can speak to important, influential people like that. Besides, he's too busy.'

Then an idea came into her mind.

'If only I could squeeze through the crowd and touch his clothes,' she thought, 'I would be healed.'

There were about 25 metres of crowd between Doris and Jesus. But she was determined to reach him somehow!

'Excuse me, please!' Doris said, very politely to start with, as she tried to work her way through the crowd.

Then she progressed to 'Mind the way', and then 'I'm coming through'. Finally, she just pushed for all she was worth, so valuable was the prize at the end—just like in a rugby scrum, where all the players are determined to reach the ball.

At last, Jesus was almost within touching distance. Doris pushed and she reached out and she pushed again and she stretched as far as she could. Eventually her fingers just touched the edge of Jesus' clothes. And immediately, she could feel that her body had been healed. But before she could jump for joy, Jesus turned round.

'Who touched me?' he asked.

His friends laughed.

'What do you mean, "Who touched me?" There are hundreds of people, all pushing and shoving round you,' they said, almost making fun of him.

But Jesus knew what he meant. Despite everyone pushing and shoving, asking questions, wanting to be healed, Doris' touch —believing that she would receive healing— hadn't gone unnoticed. Just like prayer, really!

Doris admitted what she had done, a little fearfully. But Jesus just smiled and told her that because of her faith, she had been healed.

33

Thinking about others

Teacher's information

 Bible reference

The story is based on Mark 10:32–45.

 Theme

Jesus' life on earth is an example of serving others so selflessly that, in this story, he is heading to Jerusalem to meet his death.

 Key verse

'The Son of Man did not come to be a slave master, but a slave who will give his life to rescue many people.'
MARK 10:45

 Talk about…

Ways in which we can be selfish.

 Aim

Not to put ourselves first all the time.

Jigsaw puzzled

Dear God…
Is it all right to seek fame and importance?

 Activitime

Four or five volunteers are needed to act out a visit from a member of the royal family, a well-known singer or some other VIP.

 Jigsaw piece

This incident takes place as Jesus and his disciples are travelling to Jerusalem for the Passover feast. It won't be long before Jesus is betrayed by Judas Iscariot.

Prayback

Gracious God,
Thank you that Jesus set us the example of being like a servant and not always putting ourselves first. Please help us not to live our lives with the sole intention of becoming rich, famous and important, but make us thoughtful and generous towards others at all times. In Jesus' name. Amen

Me first

'All we seem to do these days is walk, walk, walk,' one of Jesus' friends moaned, as he sat down and took off his sandals to inspect his aching feet. 'I feel as if I've done a marathon.'

The smell was so bad that a passing fly was overcome by it and fell to the ground, stunned.

'I'm more worried about what Jesus said—about who will enter his kingdom,' another replied gloomily. 'What if I'm rich one day?' The others giggled at the thought of him ever becoming rich.

'How are you going to get rich?' one of his colleagues asked. 'Selling camelburgers and fries?'

'Cheer up, lads,' a passer-by shouted as he spotted the long faces.

Jesus smiled. He was deep in thought about what was to happen to him soon.

Jesus and his friends were on their way to celebrate the Passover feast. It was the time when they would remember God saving the

firstborn sons of the Israelites from death, during one of the plagues in Egypt. The tradition for the people, at that time and place, was to make an annual pilgrimage to Jerusalem for this special occasion.

Just after Jesus and his friends had begun their journey, a discussion had arisen about who would enter God's kingdom. To everyone's surprise, Jesus had said that rich people wouldn't necessarily be included—quite a shock! Riches were thought to be God's reward for leading a good life.

Anyway, while everyone was walking along, Jesus suddenly called his friends over.

'I have to speak to you,' he said. 'It's something very important. We are on our way to Jerusalem…'

'We know that,' some of the group interrupted.

'Listen,' Jesus said firmly.

Everything went quiet. It was like the calm before the storm.

'I will be betrayed in Jerusalem, and sentenced to death,' Jesus told them. 'But in three days, I will rise from the dead.'

I don't know whether the men really understood what Jesus was saying, because it wasn't long before they were chatting among themselves again. James and John—Zebedee's sons—were particularly talkative.

'You ask him,' James instructed his brother.

'No, you ask him,' John replied, giggling nervously like a small child.

And so it went on for several minutes—'No, you', 'No, you', 'No, you'—until eventually James said, 'I don't know what to say to him.'

'All right, let's do it together,' John responded, with authority. 'This is what we'll say.' He broke into a whisper so that no one else would hear.

A few minutes later, the two lads approached Jesus. 'Could we ask you a little tiny favour, please?' they asked.

'This sounds interesting,' Jesus replied. 'What is this little tiny favour?'

Reproduced with permission from *Stories to Read Aloud* published by BRF 2004 (1 84101 362 5)

'Well…' replied the two brothers. 'It's nothing much,' they continued, trying to make the favour seem a lot smaller than it really was.

'Come on,' Jesus said.

'Yes, come on,' all the others joined in, as they looked on.

John nudged James and James nudged John. 'Go on, then!' they both said together.

They paused.

'We just wondered if, when you enter your kingdom, you could give us positions of influence and authority,' they asked, smiling nervously.

'Perhaps you could invent some jobs that were just below yours, but not too low,' one of them continued. 'You could call us… umm, errr… yes, that's it, a Prime Minister and a Foreign Secretary… or something!'

The other friends of Jesus were stunned.

'Whatever are a Prime Minister and a Foreign Secretary?' they asked. 'And what makes you two more suitable for the jobs than us, anyway?'

'Are you prepared to endure hardship and suffering, if necessary?' Jesus asked the brothers.

James and John said that they were, and Jesus knew that they would end up doing so. But he explained to them that what they had asked for wasn't his to give. The two young men walked away, rather embarrassed, whispering together.

Then Jesus called all his friends round him again. He told them that God's kingdom isn't like earthly kingdoms. So many nations rule with injustice and oppression. Many rulers are only interested in having power over people, and the resulting fame, wealth and influence. But God's kingdom is based on love and service. The greatest in God's kingdom are those who constantly put others first and themselves last—making themselves the servants of others.

'Haven't you noticed, I have never taken on the role of a mighty ruler?' Jesus said. 'I have come as a servant, and soon I will give my life for others.'

No one said anything. I think they all felt humbled by Jesus' words.

It was Jesus who finally broke the silence.

'We'll soon be in Jericho,' he called out. 'Look at that crowd of people waiting for us.'

Reproduced with permission from *Stories to Read Aloud* published by BRF 2004 (1 84101 362 5)

34

God does the impossible

Teacher's information

 Bible reference

The story is taken from Mark 10:46–52.

 Theme

Jesus asks Bartimaeus what he wants Jesus to do for him.

 Key verse

Jesus asked, 'What do you want me to do for you?'
MARK 10:51

 Talk about…

What we would like to ask Jesus to do for us.

 Aim

To bring our needs to Jesus in prayer.

Jigsaw puzzled

Dear God…
Can you help me with my problems?

 Activitime

On small pieces of paper, write down anything that is causing you problems. Place all the pieces of paper into a basket, without letting anyone else look at them. Keep them for use in the prayer time. (Afterwards, the teacher should destroy the slips of paper.)

 Jigsaw piece

This incident takes place straight after the last one, when James and John made a request to Jesus. They are still travelling to Jerusalem.

Prayback

Loving God,
*   Though you don't always take our problems away, we thank you that you can help us with them. (Hold up the container with the slips of paper in it.) We bring these needs to you today. Please help us to deal with them, and please help other people across the world with the problems that they are facing. Show them that you can do the impossible. In Jesus' name. Amen*

There's something
I want to ask you

'Get out of the way, you smelly old beggar,' a rather snobby man shouted at Bartimaeus, kicking him as if he were a bag of rubbish.

Bartimaeus had been blind since birth, and this was the place where he usually begged for money, in order to live.

'You can kick me as much as you like today,' he laughed, 'because today is a special day!'

The man frowned. 'So what makes today special for a useless bag of bones like you?' he replied scornfully.

'You'll see,' Bartimaeus answered mysteriously, with a mischievous grin. 'Someone's coming who I want to meet.'

The snobby man chuckled in an irritated manner and pushed his way through the crowd at the side of the road. A large number of people had gathered in Jericho to watch all the folk go by to the Passover feast in Jerusalem. We see similar crowds on TV, gathering to view the celebrities arriving at award ceremonies.

Suddenly, there was a commotion. Everyone began to get very excited. Bartimaeus knew what this meant—Jesus was coming.

'Is it Jesus?' he asked someone next to him. 'Has the teacher and healer arrived with his friends?'

'Yes. Now be quiet,' responded an angry bystander.

'Jesus, Jesus, over here!' Bartimaeus shouted at the top of his voice. 'I must see you, please!'

Immediately, a shout came from the back of the crowd. 'Tell that silly old fool to stop making such a noise,' the voice said.

Then all round Bartimaeus, people started to push him, shove him and shout at him.

'Jesus is far too busy to bother about the likes of you,' a woman said in disgust.

But Bartimaeus was not to be deterred.

'Jesus, Jesus, over here!' he shouted, even louder than before. 'I must see you, please!'

Everything went quiet. Jesus had stopped in the road, and so had everyone else behind him—after a few bumps because of the suddenness of the halt.

'Someone's calling me,' Jesus said to his friends.

Reproduced with permission from *Stories to Read Aloud* published by BRF 2004 (1 84101 362 5)

'There are thousands of people calling your name,' one of his friends said, a little sarcastically.

Jesus looked across the road.

'It's that blind beggar who's calling,' he said. 'Go and bring him to me, please.'

The men shouted over to Bartimaeus.

'Come on over here!' they yelled. 'Jesus wants to see you!'

Bartimaeus got up so quickly that he tripped over his big coat, but he wasn't even tempted to say a naughty word.

'Who needs coats?' he shouted, throwing it to the ground.

He ran precariously over to where the voices had come from, tripping up a few times and bumping into quite a lot of bystanders.

'Why were you calling me?' Jesus said softly. 'What do you want me to do for you?'

Bartimaeus was getting a bit choked up. He felt that one of his life's ambitions was about to be fulfilled.

'I want to be able to see,' he told Jesus.

The crowd held their breath to see what Jesus would do.

'You will see,' Jesus said gently. 'Your faith has healed you.'

As quick as a flash, Bartimaeus could see— the colours that he had never seen before, trees and houses that he had never seen before… He went round gazing into people's faces, leaping about like a two-year-old. He was so happy!

'Oh, thank you, Jesus,' he said, with tears of joy flowing down his rugged cheeks. 'I can see.'

With that, Bartimaeus followed Jesus up the street, praising God for what he'd done.

Reproduced with permission from *Stories to Read Aloud* published by BRF 2004 (1 84101 362 5)

Stories from the New Testament

———————— Luke's Gospel ————————

35

The birth of a very special baby

Teacher's information

 Bible reference

The story is based on Luke 2:1–20.

 Theme

The words that the angels speak suggest that the baby has come with a very important mission.

 Key verse

'Praise God in heaven! Peace on earth to everyone who pleases God.'
LUKE 2:14

 Talk about…

What we are celebrating on 25 December.

 Aim

To appreciate the real meaning of Christmas.

Jigsaw puzzled

Dear God…
Why was that first Christmas so important?

 Activitime

Make a Christmas card. Divide the front into four sections, similar to some picture postcards, showing four aspects of Christmas.

 Jigsaw piece

Right through the Old Testament, God's people looked forward to the coming of someone special—someone who would, in some way, save them from the effects of evil in the world. Many people in the Old Testament spoke about the circumstances of this person's birth. Jesus, God's Son, fulfils all their prophecies.

Prayback

Heavenly Father,
Thank you for sending your Son Jesus as a baby, to live on this earth among ordinary people. Thank you that, as an adult, he taught us more about you and set us an example of how to live our lives, and that now he helps us in the fight against wrongdoing and evil. Please help us never to forget that Christmas is special, because of Jesus. In Jesus' name. Amen

Moo—moo—baa— coo—zzzzzz!

'Ohhhhhh!' Blodwyn the cow sighed, as she scratched her neck vigorously on the beam of the shed.

'Do you mind?' George the ox said rather crossly. 'Some of us are trying to sleep.'

'I'm sure, if the shed was kept cleaner, you wouldn't be itching,' Hilda the goat commented. 'You've got lice.'

'Excuse me, dear!' Blodwyn argued indignantly. 'I don't have lice. It's an allergy that I have. I'm allergic to the evening air.'

'Likely story,' Cyril the dove cooed. 'Everyone knows that cows have lice.'

'Please!' Jack the donkey interrupted.

There was a moment's silence. Then Blodwyn began to scratch again. She scratched so hard that the shed seemed to shake. Cyril put his head under his wing, in search of peace. Hilda began to chew at a rope halter that was hanging on the door. And Jack stamped his foot angrily on the floor as a fly tickled his leg.

'Go to sleep!' George shouted.

'My neck is beginning to itch now,' Hilda moaned.

'Oh, for goodness' sake!' George yelled, his forehead twitching menacingly.

Jack tut-tutted, irritated by the whole situation.

Everything went silent again—that is, except for the faint hum of people bustling along the nearby street. Suddenly, just as the animals were beginning to settle down, young John, the stable lad, came in. He was carrying a pile of fresh straw and a pitchfork. After quickly scattering the straw around the floor, he rushed out.

'Strange,' Jack muttered.

'Very strange,' George agreed.

'Must be something special,' Blodwyn added.

'Coo!' was all that Cyril could think of to say.

Sure enough, a few minutes later, a middle-aged man and a young woman made their way into the stable with their donkey.

'That's all I need,' Jack moaned, 'another donkey to argue with.'

'Go to sleep!' all the other animals shouted together.

At last, everyone settled down and the animals went off to sleep. They each began to dream about the different things that animals dream about. Then suddenly, they woke up to the sound of a baby crying.

'Whatever next?' Blodwyn said, hiding a maternal smile.

KNOCK, KNOCK, KNOCK!

'Can we come in?' a group of shepherds asked.

Reproduced with permission from *Stories to Read Aloud* published by BRF 2004 (1 84101 362 5)

36

God's power over creation

Teacher's information

 ### Bible reference

The story is based on Luke 8:22–25.

 ### Theme

With Jesus in the boat, his friends (the disciples) are saved from the storm.

 ### Key verse

So they went to Jesus and woke him up, 'Master, Master! We are about to drown!' Jesus got up and ordered the wind and waves to stop. They obeyed, and everything was calm.
LUKE 8:24

? Talk about…

What we do in difficult situations.

 ### Aim

To remember that Jesus is always with us and will help us in all situations, when we follow him.

Jigsaw puzzled

Dear God…
What can I do when I feel I can't cope?

 ### Activitime

Using a selection of leaves, twigs, wool and offcuts of material or pieces of coloured paper, make a collage of a boat at sea in a storm. Imagine that the boat in the storm represents times when you find it difficult to cope. Place two figures in the boat—one is you. After the story, fill in the name of the other person who is with you and can help you on such occasions.

 ### Jigsaw piece

This is one of the most memorable of Jesus' miracles.

Prayback

Lord Jesus,
Thank you that when we trust you, we are never alone. Even when we face situations that we find hard to deal with, you are there with us, ready to help. Please help us to remember to pray about those times. In Jesus' name. Amen

A rough journey

'Oh dear!' Jesus said in a very loud voice, as he yawned a big yawn. 'It's been a busy few days and I feel ready for forty winks.'

'It's a lovely day for a sail across the lake,' one of his friends commented, as he settled himself down in the boat.

Jesus and his friends had decided to have a trip on the water, partly because it was the best way to get to where they were going and partly because it just seemed like a good idea. As they pushed the boat away from the shore, the sun was shining and the water was calm. Everyone settled down to relax and sunbathe.

As the boat slowly worked its way across the water in the gentle breeze, a contented snoring was heard in the background. Jesus had fallen asleep. He looked so peaceful. One of his friends took out his *Galilean Fisherman's Times* and began to read about the price of fish. Some of the others just leaned back and put on their sunglasses, ready to lap up the sunshine.

'Well, this is very nice,' was the comment that came from the front of the boat. And indeed it was… until things began to get a bit choppy.

Suddenly, some of the men started to turn a little green.

'It seems to be getting a bit rough,' one of them said grimly.

'Whose idea was it to go for a nice little boat trip?' another asked.

By this time, several of them were hanging over the side of the boat.

'Actually, it was Jesus' idea,' came the reply.

Talking of Jesus, he was still fast asleep on the seat at the back of the boat.

The sea got rougher. The gentle breeze turned into a gale-force wind. The boat began to toss and turn, and the waves started crashing over the top of the sail.

The men found themselves having to hold on to the sides of the vessel for dear life. Those who had been hanging over the side were now very green and had long since watched their fish-and-chip lunch disappear overboard. Jesus still hadn't stirred.

Reproduced with permission from *Stories to Read Aloud* published by BRF 2004 (1 84101 362 5)

'Enough is enough!' one of the men shouted, trying to be heard above the noise of the storm. 'Let's all shout "help", as loudly as we can, to wake Jesus up.'

After counting to three, very quickly because everyone was so frightened, they all shouted, 'Help!' As Jesus stirred, one of the men scrambled over to him and shook him violently by the shoulder.

'We're going to drown! Don't you care?' he yelled.

Jesus opened one eye, then the other. He got up slowly and held his arms up in the air.

'Enough!' he shouted to the storm, with authority.

Suddenly, the lake was calm, the wind and waves died down and the men who had spent much of the trip hanging over the side of the boat felt a lot better.

'Now,' Jesus said, 'what were you saying?'

Everyone was speechless. They just looked at each other, shrugging their shoulders and shaking their heads.

'Fancy being afraid, when you've got me in the boat!' Jesus said, smiling kindly.

All his friends felt a bit like naughty schoolchildren. They sat down, hanging their heads low and pouting a little bit.

Jesus wanted his friends to realize that they would never be alone. He would always be with them, either in person or through the Holy Spirit. If they had faith during difficult situations, he would help them through those times. After all, Jesus is God's Son, and God has power over all creation.

37

Jesus loves each one of us

Teacher's information

 Bible reference

The story is based on Luke 15:1–7.

 Theme

Whenever we say 'sorry' to Jesus for the wrong things that we have done, and are reunited with God because of that, there will be rejoicing in heaven—the lost have been found!

 Key verse

Jesus said, 'In the same way there is more happiness in heaven because of one sinner who turns to God than over ninety-nine good people who don't need to.'
LUKE 15:7

 Talk about…

Times when we have lost things—how we felt and what we did.

 Aim

To experience the love of Jesus in his forgiveness.

Jigsaw puzzled

Dear God…
Am I really important to you?

 Activitime

Organize some kind of treasure hunt—either laying a series of clues leading to the treasure, or just hiding some small objects for the members of the group to look for.

 Jigsaw piece

This is one of a group of three parables that Jesus told about finding things or people that are lost. In the story, the shepherd represents Jesus and the sheep represent us. It is a parable about Jesus' love for us, his desire to forgive, and the relationship he has with those who follow him.

Prayback

Jesus, the good shepherd,
*   Thank you for your wonderful love, expressed in your desire to forgive us for all the things that we have done wrong. Thank you that, through receiving that forgiveness, we can be friends with God. Please give everyone the desire to be forgiven by you and reunited with God.*
Amen

Let's party

I don't know if you have ever noticed, but the Bible seems to have a lot to say about sheep and shepherds. One of the best-known stories that Jesus tells is all about a shepherd. Let's call him Thomas.

Now Thomas loved his sheep. He spent hours making a fuss of them—stroking them, talking to them, and even singing to them.

His day started very early in the morning, when he'd get up and take his sheep out to find some good pasture for them to graze on. Often it would be quite late before he arrived home and put his sheep in their pen for the night.

He didn't use dogs to drive his sheep. He would just walk in front, calling them, and they would follow—they were like family pets. Sometimes, Thomas had to kill ferocious animals that came after his flock. He'd do anything for his sheep!

Anyway, one day, after Thomas had had a very long day with the sheep, he arrived home, to be met by his neighbour.

'Good day, Thomas?' he asked.

'Not too bad, thank you, Sid,' Thomas replied to his neighbour.

'Ready for your tea, I expect,' Sid continued.

'I could eat a camel,' the dedicated shepherd said. 'But first I have to count the sheep in. Woolly, one; Patch, two; Spot, three; Blackie, four; Dilys, five; Powder-puff, six; Hearth-rug, seven…

'… Daisy, ninety-seven; Muncher, ninety-eight; Cottontop, ninety-nine; and… where is Fluffy?'

'Ninety-nine is near enough, mate,' Sid comforted him. 'You've only lost one today.'

But while Sid was talking, Thomas was already heading back the way he had come, to search for the lost sheep.

'Hey, wait for me, Thomas,' Sid shouted as he ran to catch up.

They trudged through the dark and cold of the night, calling out to Fluffy. They looked behind trees and bushes. They looked into streams. They climbed hills. They walked down into valleys. They searched the highways, and they searched the byways. But Fluffy was nowhere to be seen.

'Maybe she's been eaten by a large,

ferocious, hungry animal,' Sid suggested helpfully—or not.

Both men looked so funny, covered in mud, with bits of bush sticking out from their hair—more like commandos than shepherds.

'I'm not giving up yet,' Thomas replied, with determination.

Suddenly, Sid jumped and began to tremble uncontrollably. In the light of the moon, he pointed to a very large shadow a few yards in front of them.

'It's coming to get us!' he shouted. 'There's a large, ferocious, hungry animal over there!'

Both men froze.

'What's that terrible noise?' Thomas whispered in Sid's ear.

Sid listened carefully before replying.

'Oh, that's nothing,' he mumbled. 'It's only my teeth chattering with cold and fear.'

Thomas boldly walked towards the 'monster', leaving Sid hiding behind a bush. Then all of a sudden, he heard a very familiar sound… 'Baa'.

'It's OK!' Thomas shouted. 'It's only Fluffy. She was caught up in a thorn bush, tired out from struggling.'

'You silly old girl,' a very pleased Thomas reassured Fluffy as he lifted her on to his shoulders to carry her home.

'Isn't she a bit smelly to have on your shoulders, Thomas?' Sid enquired.

'Oh yes, and very heavy!' Thomas answered.

'You must love your sheep a lot, that's all I can say,' Sid commented.

There was no reply, but it was obvious that Sid was right.

At last, they arrived home.

'I expect you're ready for bed now. I certainly am,' Sid said, yawning.

'Not at all!' a jubilant Thomas exclaimed. 'We're going to *party*!'

Reproduced with permission from *Stories to Read Aloud* published by BRF 2004 (1 84101 362 5)

38

The depth of God's love for us

Teacher's information

Bible reference

The story is based on Luke 15:11–32.

Theme

The father is waiting with open arms and forgiveness in his heart when his son returns.

Key verse

The younger son got up and started back to his father. But when he was still a long way off, his father saw him and felt sorry for him. He ran to his son and hugged and kissed him.
LUKE 15:20

Talk about…

Things that make us happy and things that make us sad.

Aim

To find real joy in doing God's will and accepting his love for us.

Jigsaw puzzled

Dear God…
Can I be happy all the time?

Activitime

Draw a smiley face and underneath write something that makes you happy. Then draw a sad face and underneath write something that makes you sad.

Jigsaw piece

This is another parable that Jesus told. It's about the depth of God's love for us all. The father in the story represents God. We are his children.

Prayback

Heavenly Father,
Thank you that you love us so much, even when we disobey you and turn our backs on you. Please help us to realize that real lasting joy can only be found when we are obedient to you and accept your love—through following Jesus. In Jesus' name. Amen

Home, sweet home

Before I start this story, I would like to point out that there is a difference between happiness and joy. Happiness is that nice feeling that we get when everything seems to be going well, but it can soon be destroyed when things go wrong. Joy, on the other hand, is a deeper feeling of warmth and peace inside that remains intact even when we go through difficult or sad times. This story is all about a young man who, in looking for happiness, found joy.

Once upon a time, long, long ago in a far-off land, there lived a man who had two sons. How's that for a dramatic opening to the story? Anyway, the man's two sons were like chalk and cheese. The elder was a hard-working, loyal, conscientious lad. The younger just wanted to have a good time.

The father wanted what was best for his two sons. He loved them very much and he had built up a large farm that would be theirs one day. Having said that, he had a hard job trying to keep his younger son in order, and it was not unusual for disagreements to arise.

One day, the younger son went to his poor old dad—with attitude!

'I want to talk to you, right now!' the son demanded.

'What is it, son?' the father asked compassionately. 'What would you like to say?'

The boy frowned.

'I do wish you wouldn't always be so kind and understanding,' he continued. 'Can't you see that I'm angry?'

'I'll try to do something about it,' the father replied affectionately.

'It doesn't matter now, anyway,' the younger son snapped. 'I only wanted to say that I'm fed up with living at home. "Be in at ten… Tidy your bedroom… Help on the farm… Clean the camel…" I want to be happy. *I'm leaving home!'*

The father was about to offer to pack his lunch… but then had second thoughts.

'And what's more,' the younger son continued, 'I need my share of the family money immediately.'

The father was very upset. But he knew that there were certain lessons that the boy would only learn from experience. One of them was that we can't have happiness all the time, and sometimes, the more we look for happiness, the less we find it. So, reluctantly, the father gave the boy his money and let him go.

At first, life was great for the lad—travel, parties, a new top-of-the-range camel with air-conditioning and anti-lock brakes, diamond-studded sandals… and he had lots of friends. Happiness!

But then the money ran out.

'Doesn't bother me,' the young man said to himself. 'I've got lots of friends who will help me out.'

What friends? It was as if he'd got the plague!

Reproduced with permission from *Stories to Read Aloud* published by BRF 2004 (1 84101 362 5)

All his so-called friends suddenly disappeared when they realized that the money had run out.

'No problem,' the lad said to himself. 'Over to plan B. I'll get a job.'

However, jobs were scarce, so he ended up looking after pigs. The young lad wasn't treated very well. He had to live outside with the pigs and he had very little to eat. He wasn't even allowed to have any of the pigs' food.

While the father's younger son was sitting out with the pigs one day, not very happy, he began to realize how incredibly stupid he had been. He thought about how fortunate he had been at home. Yet he'd run away, squandered all his money and found some awful friends before coming to that realization. He stood up excitedly.

'I'm going home,' he announced to the pigs.

The pigs just kept on rooting about as the young man raced down the road, skipping and singing. Passers-by looked on in astonishment. He was acting as if he'd just won a world cruise in a competition, or something like that.

While the lad journeyed home, he prepared a little 'sorry' speech for his dad. But he didn't need it. His father happened to be looking out of the window when his younger son walked across the fields towards home. He was so overjoyed that the boy didn't get a chance to do his little speech.

Before the lad got his breath back, the whole village had arrived for a huge barbecue to celebrate his return. That is, all except for his brother, who was a bit cross because his little brother, after squandering half the family fortune, was getting a party.

'Come on, son,' the father said to the elder boy. 'Your brother's home. Surely that's worth celebrating?'

Having searched for happiness, the younger son had found joy in his own home through his father's love. He was a very forgiving father, that's all I can say. Could anyone love their children as much as that? Well, I know someone who does… *God does!*

39

Hell

Teacher's information

Bible reference

The story is based on Luke 16:19–31.

Theme

The rich man dies and goes to hell.

Key verses

The poor man died, and angels took him to the place of honour next to Abraham. The rich man also died and was buried. He went to hell and was suffering terribly. When he looked up and saw Abraham far off and Lazarus at his side, he said to Abraham, 'Have pity on me! Send Lazarus to dip his finger in water and touch my tongue. I'm suffering terribly in this fire.'
LUKE 16:22–24

Talk about...

What it would be like to live in a place where God's love was not present.

Aim

To listen to the message of scripture and make wise choices.

Jigsaw puzzled

Dear God...
Is there really a place called 'hell'?

Activitime

Write the word 'WARNING' in large letters along the top of, or diagonally across, a fairly large sheet of paper. At the end of the story, make it into a poster telling people why hell is not a nice place to go to.

Jigsaw piece

Jesus told many parables. This is one of the less well-known ones, which talks about hell.

Prayback

God of love and hope,
Thank you that you sent Jesus to us so that, through trusting in him, we can be assured of a home in heaven and be in your presence for ever. Please help people not to be like the rich man in the story, who made the wrong choices and ended up in hell. In Jesus' name. Amen

Could I have a drink?

There once lived a man who was rich... very rich... very, very rich. He had everything that money could buy—camels, sheep, goats, silver and gold ornaments... No, let's start again and bring this story up to date!

Roderick Money-Love was a multi-millionaire. He was the chairman of a multi-national company that sold computer software. He had started off in a very small way, selling computer games on a market stall, and it had all grown from there.

Many would say that what Roderick Money-Love hadn't got wasn't worth having. Apart from having a selection of six mansions around the world, Roderick had his own yacht, a private plane, a fleet of limousines and sports cars, and a string of racehorses. He was unhappily married and his children despised him.

Mr Money-Love employed thousands of people, including his gardener, Mr Lazarus. Mr Lazarus was very poor because his employer paid him such a low wage. He never had very good health because Mr Money-Love wouldn't give him the time off work to have an important operation that could cure the problem.

Mr Lazarus begged his boss for more money and time off for his medical treatment, but his pleadings were just ignored. Eventually, Mr Lazarus' condition got so bad that he died, and there wasn't even enough money to give him a proper funeral.

Roderick continued to eat, drink and be merry. He put on too much weight, smoked too much and ended up with clogged arteries through the wrong kind of diet and lifestyle.

One day, quite suddenly, he died of a heart attack. It was very quick, really. He moaned and groaned a bit, got breathless, clutched his chest and that was that. Despite all his earthly wealth, his life couldn't be saved by the doctors and nurses. And what's more, he couldn't take his money or possessions with him—you're not allowed to!

You might think that that was the end of the story. Both men were dead and buried. But oh no! We're eternal beings—even though we die physically, that is not the end.

Because he had been a follower of Jesus and had lived according to God's word in the Bible, Mr Lazarus went to heaven. He was able to enjoy living in God's wonderful presence for ever, surrounded by his love and blessings.

Roderick Money-Love, on the other hand, had decided to ignore Jesus and the Bible, so he went to hell. He had to endure living in the absence of God's love for ever. In hell, there is no love, no goodness, no beauty, no joy, no peace, no comfort, no healing or wholeness, no hope—it must be a horrible place to be in!

Roderick shouted out for help. He hoped that someone would relieve his suffering. He would have given anything for even a glass of cool water—but no one would give him anything. Then he called out to the Old Testament prophet Abraham, who was in heaven.

'Could you at least send Mr Lazarus back to my father's house, to tell my brothers how awful it is to live here?' he pleaded. 'It's like... well, it's not really like anything I've ever known. It's indescribably awful!'

But Abraham knew that it would be a waste of time. Sadly, there will always be some people who will choose to ignore Jesus until it is too late!

40

Taking God for granted

Teacher's information

 ### Bible reference

The story is based on Luke 17:11–19.

 ### Theme

After Jesus has healed the ten lepers, only one comes back to thank God.

 ### Key verse

'Why was this foreigner the only one who came back to thank God?'
LUKE 17:18

 ### Talk about…

Things that God has done for us.

 ### Aim

To remember to say 'thank you' to God.

Jigsaw puzzled

Dear God…
Does it matter if we forget to say 'thank you'?

 ### Activitime

Make a 'thank you' card for someone who has given something to you or done something to help you, and give the card to them.

 ### Jigsaw piece

This miracle of Jesus takes place on the border between Samaria and Galilee. The interesting aspect is the response of the ten people after they have been healed.

Prayback

God who answers prayer,
Thank you for all the wonderful things that you give to us and do for us. Thank you for the prayers that you have answered and for all the wonderful promises that you have made to us in the Bible. Please help us not to forget to thank you. In Jesus' name. Amen

Oops! I forgot

Jesus was on his way to Jerusalem. His friends were with him, but they were busy chatting among themselves. It was a lovely bright day, there was just a gentle breeze and the countryside looked lovely.

'Ah, peace and quiet,' Jesus said to himself, with a sigh.

Don't get me wrong—Jesus loved to do his Father's work, but he did get tired and he did need some quiet time as well.

After a while, they reached a village. But just as Jesus was about to enter it, followed by his friends, they heard someone calling.

'Jesus, we need your help. Please help us!' came several voices in unison.

One of Jesus' friends turned round to the others.

'Who said that?' he asked, squinting in the sun, looking for some response.

Then the voices came again.

'Jesus, we need your help. Please help us!'

The man frowned as he looked at the others.

'Has one of you been learning ventriloquism?' he enquired. 'I heard the words, but no one's lips moved!'

One of the others let his head go floppy and his mouth drop open, just like a ventriloquist's dummy. They all laughed together at the impression, but then one of them suddenly pointed to something in the distance. It was a group of people—rather scruffy-looking people. They looked as if they hadn't had a wash for weeks and their clothes reminded the men of old floorcloths.

'That's where the voices are coming from,' another of the friends confirmed.

As they got closer, Jesus and his friends could see the sad truth. They were a group of ten lepers.

'Look at those poor people with leprosy,' Jesus said softly and with compassion.

His friends could see their dry, scaly skin and the stubs of fingers and arms that had been eaten away as a result of the disease. The lepers had had to leave their families so that they wouldn't pass the disease on to them.

'Are you going to heal them?' Jesus' friends asked.

He smiled as he shouted across to the

group. 'Go and show yourselves to the priests,' he told them.

It was the law in those days that, before lepers were allowed home, they had to be inspected by a priest to say that they were cured.

The lepers believed that they would be healed by the time they saw the priest, so they began their journey. Then suddenly, one of them cried out.

'I'm healed! I'm healed! I'm healed!' he shouted. 'Look at my skin. It's like a baby's skin! Look at my arms and hands. I've got fingers and thumbs again!'

'Me too!' yelled another and another and another…

Yet another shouted, 'What are we waiting for? Let's go to the priest!'

One of the men turned back in the direction that they had come from.

'Where are you going?' the others asked. 'We've got to go to the priest so that we can see our wives and children again.'

'I want to give my little girl a big hug,' one of the men added, with tears in the corners of his eyes.

'I want to see my wife and children—of course I do,' answered the man who had turned back, 'and I want to hold them. But first of all, I'm going to say "thank you" to Jesus.'

There was a moment's silence.

'Well, you needn't think that we're coming with you,' the others jeered, as they continued on their journey.

The one leper eventually caught up with Jesus.

'Thank you, Jesus, I'm healed. Praise and thanks to God,' he yelled at the top of his voice.

'Where are all the others?' Jesus asked. 'Aren't they going to thank God as well?'

The man didn't know what to say. He could feel his face going as red as a beetroot. Jesus smiled. He knew it wasn't the man's fault.

'Go to the priest and then return to your family,' Jesus instructed him. 'God has made you well.'

The man raced off up the road. Jesus could see him waving his arms and leaping with joy until, eventually, he was just a tiny black dot in the distance.

'Let's go,' Jesus said to his friends. 'There's lots more work to be done!'

As they entered the village, they all felt good inside.

Reproduced with permission from *Stories to Read Aloud* published by BRF 2004 (1 84101 362 5)

41

We can't fool God

Teacher's information

 ### Bible reference

The story is based on Luke 18:9–14.

 ### Theme

Because he pretends that he has never done anything wrong, the Pharisee is not forgiven by God.

 ### Key verse

Then Jesus said, 'When the two men went home, it was the tax collector and not the Pharisee who was pleasing to God. If you put yourself above others, you will be put down. But if you humble yourself, you will be honoured.'
LUKE 18:14

 ### Talk about…

Things that we need to say 'sorry' for.

 ### Aim

To avoid pretending to be what we're not—especially with God.

Jigsaw puzzled

Dear God…
Does everyone need to say 'sorry'?

 ### Activitime

Let's pretend! Create a 'hot seat'. Three volunteers are needed to talk briefly on the subject 'I have never done anything wrong'. How convincing are they?

 ### Jigsaw piece

During Jesus' life on earth, he came across many people who were convinced that they had lived faultless lives. This parable of Jesus is aimed at them and others like them.

Prayback

God who knows everything,
Thank you that you know all about us. Please help us not to pretend to be what we are not—especially with you. But give us the courage and honesty to say 'sorry' for the things that we do wrong. In Jesus' name. Amen

Let's pretend

'Tell us another story!' a young man shouted.

Jesus spent a moment looking around at everyone, with compassion and love. There were old and young, fat and thin, tall and short, rich and poor—and dotted among the multitude of people were many who were unwell. In the distance, Jesus could see some young mums with babies and small children. They were walking towards the large crowd that had gathered. Then his eyes focused on a small group within the crowd. They were also looking around, but not with compassion or love.

'Look at all these common, wicked, miserable paupers,' one of the small group commented. 'I'm so glad that I am not like them.'

The others nodded.

'Can we go now and mix with some folk who are more our class?' another responded, looking down her nose at those around her. 'I wouldn't like to catch anything.'

'Oh mind, there's a rather smelly person walking by,' cried yet another, as he flinched and tried to escape the crowd.

'Look behind you!' shouted the first. But it was too late!

'That's it,' Jesus thought. 'Listen carefully,' he said in a loud voice. 'I've got another story.'

And this is how the story went…

One bright and sunny afternoon, two men went into the temple to pray.

One of them was a Pharisee. Now the Pharisees were a religious group who loved to tell people what to do. They believed that they were much better behaved than everyone else and that God would give them greater blessings because of that. They didn't like Jesus at all.

The other man was a tax collector. I'm afraid that tax collectors, in New Testament times, were 'bad news'—they got a very bad press. They were renowned for being dishonest—lying and cheating and swindling everyone that they could.

Yet Jesus loved to have lunch or tea with tax collectors, because God loved them. In fact, God loved them as much as he loved everyone else—and it has to be said, in general, they made no pretences about being perfect.

The Pharisee marched boldly into the temple, trying to look very holy. He stood up in the most prominent place he could find, where everyone could see him, and he began to say his prayers at the top of his voice. Everyone stared at him, which was just what he wanted.

'I've come here, God, to thank you for making me such a fine citizen—a credit to you and my family,' he began. 'I could have been a robber. I could have been lazy. I could have done things that are against your laws. I could have been like that evil tax collector over

Reproduced with permission from *Stories to Read Aloud* published by BRF 2004 (1 84101 362 5)

there. But no, you made me a perfect example to others. Amen.'

The Pharisee smiled in a very satisfied manner. He looked like the cat that had got the cream!

The poor tax collector, on the other hand, found a quiet corner where he would be unnoticed by other people. He knelt down and began to pray.

'God, have mercy on me!' he cried out. 'I have done so many things that are wrong, and I am so sorry. Please, oh please, forgive me!'

Jesus smiled and looked at the crowd.

'You know what?' he said. 'The tax collector's prayer was answered. God had mercy on him and forgave him.'

'But what about the Pharisee?' a young woman called out. 'He would have been all right, wouldn't he? Because he hadn't done anything wrong, had he?'

'Oh dear!' Jesus replied. 'Of course the Pharisee had done things that were wrong. Everyone has! His problem was that his whole life was a pretence. He managed to fool other people into thinking that he was perfect, but he couldn't fool God. He didn't say "sorry", so he wasn't forgiven.'

The small group within the crowd shuffled away, trying not to be noticed.

'I didn't like that story,' one of them mumbled.

The others nodded in agreement.

'Although,' the first person added, 'I'm sure the story couldn't have applied to us in any way.'

Oh yes, it does!

Reproduced with permission from *Stories to Read Aloud* published by BRF 2004 (1 84101 362 5)

42

Jesus came to change people's lives

Teacher's information

 Bible reference

The story is based on Luke 19:1–10.

 Theme

The evidence of Zacchaeus' life having been changed, by meeting Jesus, is there for all to see.

 Key verse

Later that day Zacchaeus stood up and said to the Lord, 'I will give half of my property to the poor. And I will now pay back four times as much to everyone I have ever cheated.'
LUKE 19:8

 Talk about...

How greed affects people.

 Aim

To know that Jesus still changes lives today—for the better!

Jigsaw puzzled

Dear God...
Can you make me a better person?

 Activitime

Bring some loose change and have a collection for charity. Discuss which charity to give the money to.

Jigsaw piece

This is the account of how, in Jericho, a man's life was transformed through meeting with Jesus.

Prayback

Life-changing Lord Jesus,
Thank you that your work on earth was all about changing lives for the better. Thank you that you still do that. Please help us to live better lives, and help those who feel that something is wrong, like the little man in the story, to meet with you.
Amen

What's new?

There once lived a short man—a very short man. He didn't like being short, because when anything special happened anywhere and the crowds gathered, he could never see over the top of them. Apart from that, people used to make fun of him. They would call him names, like 'Titch' or 'Shorty'.

Mind you, nobody liked him anyway because he was a tax collector. He worked for the Romans in Jericho and was not very honest. He always charged too much tax and then pocketed the extra. He lived a quiet life, keeping himself to himself—because he had no friends. Most of his spare time he spent counting all his money. And that took him quite a while!

One day, there was a commotion in the street outside the little man's house. Crowds were pushing and shoving and talking excitedly. The little man rushed out, coat in hand, one sandal on his foot and the other shoved in his pocket to put on later.

'What's happening?' he asked. But everyone ignored him, just as if he wasn't there.

'What's happening? Who's coming?' he enquired, in a louder voice.

But still no one replied. Suddenly, he tripped over something and fell. As he lay sprawled across the path, he looked up and saw what he had fallen over. It was a board with a poster on it: 'Buy your copy of the *Jericho Express* today. Read about Jesus coming to town'.

The little man scrambled to his feet excitedly. Jesus was famous: he healed people who were unwell, fed people who were hungry and told wonderful stories.

'Perhaps Jesus could do something for me,' he thought—because the little man was really quite miserable.

'Let me see! Let me see!' the little man shouted, pushing and shoving, trying to get to the front of the crowd. But it was hopeless.

Then suddenly, he had a brainwave. 'If I could just climb that tree…' he thought to himself.

It was a bit of a struggle. He tore his coat and scratched his knee, but eventually managed to get high enough up the tree to get a good view. He looked ever so funny, perched on a branch.

'Look at me!' he shouted smugly. 'I can see better than any of you now.'

But the crowds took no notice of him—still.

'Here comes Jesus!' came a distant shout.

The woman in front of the tree craned her neck forward in order to see. Sure enough, Jesus was coming. The little man leaned over to get a good view and nearly lost his balance.

Then, to his surprise, as Jesus was passing by he looked up into the tree and asked, 'Zacchaeus, have you got something nice for tea? I'd love to come and eat with you.'

The little man was so surprised that he didn't know what to say, so he quietly muttered to himself, 'That's *my* name. I'm Zacchaeus, and what's more, Jesus wants to come to *my* house for tea.'

Then, a bit louder and very excitedly, he repeated, 'Jesus wants to come to my house for tea.'

Then, at the top of his voice, he yelled, 'I'm just coming! Don't go away. Let's go and have tea.'

Zacchaeus may have climbed up the tree slowly, but he came down like a monkey.

Zacchaeus was so excited that he grabbed Jesus by the arm and almost dragged him across the road into his house. Mouths dropped—people in the crowd couldn't believe it.

'He's a sinner! Jesus is going to eat with a sinner!' someone called out.

An hour or two later, the crowd was even more shocked when Zacchaeus came out and started giving his money away. He told everyone that he wanted to give back what he had stolen, and also help the poor.

'I wouldn't have believed it if I hadn't seen it with my own two eyes,' commented a next-door neighbour.

In the meantime, Jesus had a big smile on his face. This was what his mission was all about, and still is—*changing people's lives for the better*.

Reproduced with permission from *Stories to Read Aloud* published by BRF 2004 (1 84101 362 5)

Stories from the New Testament

—— John's Gospel ——

43

God's power over death

Teacher's information

 Bible reference

The story is taken from John 11:1–44.

 Theme

At Jesus' command, Lazarus is raised from the dead.

 Key verses

When Jesus had finished praying, he shouted, 'Lazarus, come out!' The man who had been dead came out. His hands and feet were wrapped with strips of burial cloth, and a cloth covered his face. Jesus then told the people, 'Untie him and let him go.'
JOHN 11:43–44

 Talk about…

Whether or not we should be frightened about death.

 Aim

To think about what happens after we die.

Jigsaw puzzled

Dear God…
Is death the end?

 Activitime

Draw a picture showing different methods of communication these days—ways in which people can be informed of good or bad news (maybe the death of a loved one).

 Jigsaw piece

Lazarus was the brother of Martha and Mary. They were very close friends of Jesus and lived in Bethany. This is one of the most amazing miracles performed by Jesus.

Prayback

Heavenly Father,
Thank you that when we follow Jesus, we enter into a wonderful relationship with you. Thank you that even after we die, that relationship continues as we come to live in heaven. And, as a result, we don't need to fear death. Please help us, and others, to have that confidence. In Jesus' name. Amen

Too late?

A young lad came running up to Jesus one day, puffing and panting. He looked as if he had just run a marathon.

'I have a message for you, teacher. It's very urgent!' he gasped.

Jesus put his hand on the boy's shoulder.

'Get your breath back, son,' he replied kindly. 'Then you can tell me what the trouble is.'

After a few moments and a cool drink, the young man began to speak.

'I've been sent by your friends Martha and Mary, from Bethany,' he explained. 'I've come with very serious news. Lazarus is extremely ill. Everyone fears for his life.'

Jesus was very sad to hear the message and he felt concerned for the family. But he knew that God had a reason for allowing this to happen and everything would work out in the end—in God's perfect timing.

'It's all right!' Jesus said reassuringly. 'This illness will not end in death.'

Jesus' friends rushed over to him.

'What are you going to do about Lazarus?' one of them asked.

'Nothing, at the moment,' Jesus replied.

His friends were glad in a way, because there had been some trouble in Bethany when they had last been there.

It came as quite a surprise, however, when two days later Jesus announced that they were all going to see Martha, Mary and Lazarus.

'He's asleep at the moment,' Jesus said, with sadness in his voice, 'but I'm going to wake him up.'

His friends looked at each other.

'It's a long way to go to wake someone up,' one of them whispered to the others, with a bit of a grin on his face.

'If he's still ill, wouldn't it be better to let him sleep?' another of the men asked Jesus.

But of course, Jesus really meant that Lazarus had died and God was going to bring him back to life through Jesus.

Just before Jesus and his friends arrived at Bethany, Martha ran out to meet them. She wasn't just upset because her brother had died, she was upset because Jesus hadn't come earlier.

'It's too late now! Where have you been? He's dead, he's dead!' she cried, tears flowing down her face. 'But even now, nothing is impossible for God.'

Jesus was so sad. His heart went out to Martha.

'Lazarus will rise from the dead,' he assured her.

'I know that one day he will go to heaven,' she replied.

'Do you believe that everyone who follows

Reproduced with permission from *Stories to Read Aloud* published by BRF 2004 (1 84101 362 5)

me will enter into a wonderful relationship with God—one that will continue for ever?' Jesus asked.

'Yes, I do,' Martha responded, still with tears trickling down her cheeks, 'because you are the Son of God.'

As they neared Bethany, Martha ran to fetch Mary. Mary was upset as well, because Jesus had not arrived earlier. Jesus held Mary in his arms for a moment.

'Take me to Lazarus,' he said suddenly.

When they arrived at the tomb, Jesus was moved to tears. He asked some of the mourners to take away the stone that had been rolled in front of the entrance.

'The body will smell rather strong,' Martha warned. 'Lazarus has been dead for four days.'

'Don't worry about smells. God is going to demonstrate his power to you all today, with a wonderful miracle,' Jesus told her.

Once the stone had been rolled away, Jesus thanked God for what he was about to do.

Then, in a very loud voice, he called to Lazarus.

'Lazarus, it's time to come out!'

There was a stunned silence. Before people got a chance to express their doubts, they heard a noise coming from the tomb. Lazarus stumbled precariously out into the sunshine, still wrapped in the graveclothes.

'Remove the strips of linen from his head—he can't see!' Jesus told the sisters. Jesus was laughing because he was so pleased that his friend was alive again.

'And take him to get freshened up and put some proper clothes on.'

Everyone was overjoyed... well, most people were! A few of the onlookers ran to the Pharisees to tell them what had happened, and they began to plot against Jesus. You always seem to get someone who wants to cause trouble, don't you? However, it was an unforgettable occasion and many people put their trust in Jesus, having seen God's power at work through him—even over death.

44

Jesus wants to be our friend

Teacher's information

 ### Bible reference

The story is based on John 15:1–17.

 ### Theme

Jesus gave his life for his friends. We can be his friends, when we demonstrate our faith in him by doing the things that he wants us to do.

 ### Key verses

'You are my friends, if you obey me.'
JOHN 15:14

 ### Talk about…

Friendship.

 ### Aim

To understand more about our relationship with Jesus.

Jigsaw puzzled

Dear God…
What does it mean to be friends with Jesus?

 ### Activitime

Using silks, wool, coloured string or raffia, and beads, plait a friendship bracelet to give away.

 ### Jigsaw piece

This passage is part of Jesus' teaching about the kind of relationship that he wants with everyone.

Prayback

God of love,
Thank you that everyone can be friends with Jesus. Please help us to obey his teaching as evidence of our faith in him. Enable us to put our trust completely in Jesus, to be filled with his love and to allow that love to spill out on to those around us. In Jesus' name. Amen

Let's do some pruning

'Hands up, those of you who grow grapes,' Jesus asked the large crowd that had gathered round him.

Hands began to go up everywhere. One man prodded his neighbour in the ribs with his rather pointed elbow.

'Put your hand up!' he shouted out, so loudly that everyone looked round. 'You grow grapes—very sour ones!'

After an indignant look, another hand went up. Jesus smiled.

'Good,' he said. 'So you will understand what I am about to tell you now.'

Jesus must have had some gardening experience, because he was always talking about growing things. On this occasion, he spoke about vines, and what he said was common sense to those who were listening.

Jesus explained that the sensible thing to do with branches that don't produce fruit is to cut them off the vine. Then all the branches that do produce fruit are pruned, just enough to make them produce even more fruit. Any branch that is cut off the vine cannot produce fruit, because it has no nourishment.

But what threw everyone was when Jesus said, 'Listen carefully. This isn't really about gardening. It's about you and your relationship with me. I am the vine, you are the branches and my Father is the gardener.'

One old farmer looked down at his clothes and, to his surprise, found some old dead leaves clinging on to his woollen cloak. He began to brush them off, looking very worried. He visualized himself turning into a large branch.

'He doesn't mean it literally,' his wife scolded as she cuffed him playfully on the shoulder.

Others began to murmur.

'What does he mean?' they all asked each other. 'How can we be branches producing fruit?'

Some, however, remembered the parable of the farmer sowing seeds, and had understood what Jesus had meant then about producing a harvest.

'Don't you understand?' Jesus asked. 'If you don't depend on me, you won't be able to live the kind of life that I am teaching you about. And people will not be able to recognize you as my followers.'

'What shall we do?' someone shouted out.

'Love one another,' Jesus replied. 'Trust in me. Be filled with my love. And then you will have enough love to share with those around you.'

'One day, I will show you how much I love you all,' Jesus said. 'I want you all to be my friends, and you can be, if you do the things that I command you to do.'

Reproduced with permission from *Stories to Read Aloud* published by BRF 2004 (1 84101 362 5)

45

God gives new life

Teacher's information

 Bible reference

The story is based on John 20:1–18.

 Theme

Mary sees that Jesus is alive.

 Key verse

Then Jesus said to her, 'Mary!' She turned and said to him, 'Rabboni.' The Aramaic word 'Rabboni' means 'Teacher'.
JOHN 20:16

 Talk about…

What it means to have a fresh start.

 Aim

To try to be more like Jesus.

Jigsaw puzzled

Dear God…
Can Jesus help me to live a better life?

 Activitime

When we enter into a new life trusting Jesus, it means giving up things that are not pleasing to him and starting to do new things that are pleasing to him. Make two lists on a sheet of paper—a list of the type of things we should give up and a list of the type of new things we should be starting to do.

 Jigsaw piece

After Jesus' death on the cross, his followers were devastated. Although Jesus had always said that he would rise from the dead on the third day, no one really seems to be expecting it to happen.

Prayback

Living Lord Jesus,
*   You rose from the dead and are alive today! Thank you that, through following you, we too can have a fresh start. Please help us to give up the things that are not pleasing to you and start living the kind of life that you lived on earth as our example. Enable us to lead others to you so that they might experience a fresh start as well. Amen*

He's alive!

For the many followers of Jesus, it had been a very sad few days. Jesus had seemed to be so popular. Wherever he had gone, the crowds had gathered to be healed and to listen to his stories. Many people had really believed that he was the Son of God, but now he was dead—brutally killed on a cross.

When Jesus had been around, life had seemed better and it had been easier to live according to God's values. Now questions were being asked about the reality of the kingdom that Jesus had talked about.

It was early on Sunday morning. Mary Magdalene and some others had decided to go to the tomb to prepare Jesus' body properly for burial. It was so early that it was still not completely daylight as the group walked along the road in silence, tears rolling down their cheeks.

It was Mary who reached the tomb first. She strained to see in the semi-darkness and through her tears. To her surprise and horror, the large stone had already been rolled away from the entrance.

Mary raced back to Peter and John, who were also on their way to the tomb. She grabbed hold of Peter's arm, trembling.

'Mary, whatever's wrong?' he asked softly, giving her a comforting hug.

'Someone has stolen Jesus' body,' she answered, sobbing. 'Where could they have taken it?'

Mary started to head back towards the open tomb with the group, to find out what had happened.

Peter and John ran. John was faster, so he arrived first. John looked through the entrance at the discarded burial garments, but Peter, as one would expect, went right in. Peter was sometimes a bit like a bull in a china shop—act first and think later—but he meant well.

After a few moments, John also went in. As soon as he entered, he saw the full scene—the empty tomb and the abandoned graveclothes. He believed immediately that Jesus had risen from the dead. The others weren't quite so sure.

Jesus' followers hadn't realized the significance of his death on the cross, paying the penalty for sin. The reality was that he had made it possible for us all to be forgiven for the wrong things that we have done and be reunited with God.

Equally, they hadn't realized that Jesus' rising from the dead was also part of God's plan, offering a fresh start to people. Easter Day is all about new life. Jesus was raised from the dead and, because of that, when we place our trust in him and follow him, we too can have 'new life'.

It's a second chance—an opportunity to live a better life with Jesus as our friend, and to be more like him. Also, it's the hope of a home in heaven when we die.

Anyway, Peter and John returned home with a curious mixture of feelings.

'I'll stay here a little longer,' Mary told them as the others began to walk back down the road.

She still believed that Jesus' body had been stolen. Once again, she looked into the tomb, but this time she had quite a surprise. Through her tear-filled eyes, she saw two figures dressed in white. They had very kind faces. They were angels.

'Why are you so upset?' they both asked.

Mary explained what she thought had happened and, with that, she turned round. She jumped, because someone was standing behind her. Not recognizing who it was, because of the tears in her eyes, she thought it was the gardener.

'Please tell me where you have hidden Jesus' body,' she pleaded.

But it wasn't the gardener. It was Jesus, and he had risen from the dead. He just said one word in reply to the request.

'Mary.'

That was enough. He said it with such warmth and compassion, she knew exactly who it was and flung her arms round him. The tears flowed even faster. This time, they were tears of joy.

'Go and tell the others that you have seen me,' he continued.

Mary could hardly believe that Jesus had been raised from the dead… that he was alive again. She ran as fast as she could, to do what he had said. Her face was radiant as she burst into the room where Jesus' friends were.

'Do you want the good news or the bad news first?' she asked, bubbling over with joy.

She was so excited that she just couldn't stand still.

'Let's have some good news,' one of the group replied. 'We've had enough bad news lately.'

'I've seen him! I've seen Jesus! And he's alive!' Mary cried out, unable to keep it to herself any longer. 'And there is no bad news. How could there be, now that Jesus has risen from the dead?'

46

The nature of true faith

Teacher's information

 Bible reference

The story is based on John 20:19–31.

 Theme

Jesus emphasizes that part of 'true faith' is being certain of what we haven't physically seen.

 Key verse

Jesus said, 'Thomas, do you have faith because you have seen me? The people who have faith in me without seeing me are the ones who are really blessed!'
JOHN 20:29

 Talk about…

Hopes for the future—things that we can be sure will happen. The Bible tells us that 'faith makes us sure of what we hope for and gives us proof of what we cannot see' (Hebrews 11:1).

 Aim

To follow Jesus with faith.

> ### Jigsaw puzzled
>
> *Dear God…*
> *What does it mean to have faith?*

 Activitime

Either prepare a list beforehand or ask for some volunteers to share an 'incredible fact' each. Every one should sound unbelievable—but some should be true and some not. Take a vote on whether or not you believe each one.

 Jigsaw piece

This is another of Jesus' appearances after his resurrection.

> ### Prayback
>
> *Living God,*
> *   Thank you for the story of Thomas. Many of us can identify with his feelings —it's so easy to have doubts. Please give us more faith in Jesus, in you, in the Holy Spirit, and in your promises to us. And help others to have the faith to believe the Christian message as well. In Jesus' name. Amen*

I doubt that!

'I'm not spending another night shut in here,' Thomas said, as he got out of his chair.

The others looked at him, saying nothing.

'Don't look at me like that,' Thomas continued. 'We're all devastated by what's happened during the last few days, and confused by these reports that Jesus has risen from the dead. I don't know what to believe. But I just can't cope with this sitting around.'

Thomas grabbed his coat and left in a hurry.

'Where are you going?' someone shouted after him.

'I don't know,' he replied, turning round. 'I just need to get out. I feel like a bird shut up in a cage.'

Then one of the group ran to the door after him. 'Well, be careful!' he yelled.

But it was too late. Thomas had already gone. Everyone sat down again to what would be a rather interesting evening.

It was a couple of hours later when Thomas finally returned. He looked tired out, but before he had a chance to sit down, one of his friends grabbed his arm in excitement.

'What's happened?' Thomas asked rather drily.

'What's happened? What's happened?' his friend repeated, bubbling over with excitement.

Two of the men were doing a little dance round the room. Then they fell over a cushion that was lying on the floor and ended up in an untidy heap.

'We've seen him!' they all said in unison. 'We've seen him!'

'Who have you seen?' Thomas pleaded.

He was struggling to deal with life generally, struggling to keep awake and struggling to understand what was going on. Then one of his friends placed a hand on Thomas' shoulder and looked into his eyes, emphasizing the words as he spoke.

'We've seen Jesus. He appeared to us right here,' he explained.

Reproduced with permission from *Stories to Read Aloud* published by BRF 2004 (1 84101 362 5)

Thomas flopped down into the chair, shaking his head in disbelief.

'We really did,' everyone confirmed.

Thomas sat silently for two or three minutes. Everyone was waiting for some sort of comment... and then it came!

'No! No!' he shouted. 'Don't tell me things like that. I don't believe it. Unless I see Jesus for myself and am able to feel where the nails and spear went in... I will never believe it.'

'There's no more to be said, then,' one of the others replied in despair.

And that was how it was left... that is, until a week later.

Thomas and the others were in the house again. All the doors were securely locked, but suddenly Jesus was standing among them. He greeted them all affectionately. Then he turned to Thomas.

'Thomas, what am I going to do with you?' he asked, a smile on his face. 'Feel my hands where the nails went in, and feel my side where I was stabbed with the spear.'

Thomas felt the scars.

'Lord, it is you!' he shouted exuberantly, hugging Jesus.

Jesus was silent for a moment. Then he spoke. 'You only believe that I have risen from the dead because you have seen me alive and felt my scars. True faith is to believe without any kind of physical proof.'

I guess Thomas was feeling a bit guilty afterwards. In fact, maybe several of Jesus' friends were feeling a bit guilty. It's easy to believe in what we can see, touch, smell, hear or taste, but when there's a lack of physical proof, it's more difficult.

Believing that Jesus is alive today and trusting in God's promises for the future, with complete certainty, calls for 'true' faith.

Reproduced with permission from *Stories to Read Aloud* published by BRF 2004 (1 84101 362 5)

47

Jesus understands failure

Teacher's information

 ### Bible reference

The story is based on John 21:1–19.

 ### Theme

Jesus reinstates Peter, despite his failure, because of Peter's love for him.

 ### Key verse

Jesus asked a third time, 'Simon son of John, do you love me?' Peter was hurt because Jesus had asked him three times if he loved him. So he told Jesus, 'Lord, you know everything. You know I love you.' Jesus replied, 'Feed my sheep.'
JOHN 21:17

 ### Talk about...

Times when we don't live up to what we ourselves, or others, expect of us (including Jesus' expectations).

 ### Aim

To try again when we fail.

Jigsaw puzzled

Dear God...
What happens if I sometimes get things wrong?

 ### Activitime

Play 'Yes, I remember'. Ask for some volunteers to come and talk about an object that brings back memories for them (memories of a person, a place, a situation and so on).

 ### Jigsaw piece

This story takes place after a lot of activity. Following his death on the cross, Jesus was raised to life again by God. This is one of several appearances that he made after his resurrection. On this occasion, his attention was focused largely on Peter, who, after Jesus' arrest, had denied all knowledge of him three times.

Prayback

Lord Jesus,
Thank you that you gave Peter a second chance, and that you offer a fresh start to everyone who follows you. Please help us to learn from the times when we have failed to live up to your expectations of us. Enable us to love and follow you more, and guide and strengthen us to live the kind of lives that are pleasing to you. Be with others who have feelings of failure at this time. Amen

It's OK, Peter

'Do you know what I fancy doing?' Peter said one night, just after the resurrection of Jesus. Peter was with six other friends of Jesus at the time.

'What's that?' one of the others replied, smiling. 'Do you fancy going disco-dancing until the early hours of the morning—dancing the night away? I do love the Fisherman's Hornpipe. I'll…'

'No! No!' Peter interrupted. 'I fancy going fishing. Then we can have a beach barbecue. I love fish in a bun and fries.'

'Trust old Peter to be thinking about his stomach,' the others laughed together.

It had been a difficult time for the friends, but they were feeling a lot brighter now that Jesus had been raised from the dead.

They all walked over to the little wooden fishing boat.

'You get in, and I'll push the boat out,' Peter shouted over the excited chattering of his friends.

'Don't fall overboard into the water,' one of the would-be fishermen jeered at the others.

Soon they were on their way. The nets were lowered and they fished all night—but caught nothing.

'I'm hungry,' one of the crew moaned as it began to get light.

'I feel sick,' whined another. 'We've been bobbing up and down on the waves all night and now my head is spinning like a top!'

'I want to go to bed,' came the sorrowful little voice of someone at the back of the boat, his head nodding in rhythm with the rising and falling of the boat in the waves.

Peter tried to be cheerful about the whole situation. 'I needed to go on a diet anyway,' he commented, with a giggle.

Then his stomach made a loud, hollow, gurgling noise.

'It's a pity you can't convince your stomach of that,' someone quipped. And everyone laughed.

Then suddenly, from the boat they spotted a shadowy figure in the distance, on the shore. They could see that it was a man, although they couldn't make out who it was. Perhaps he sensed that it had been a bad night for the fishermen, because he made a comment.

'Have you caught anything?' he shouted across the water, with such sensitivity that it would not cause offence.

'Not a thing!' the fishermen replied together.

'Try putting your net over the right-hand side of the boat, then you'll catch something,' the stranger said.

He spoke with such authority that the fishermen obeyed without question. Immediately, the net was filled so full that it was too heavy to lift into the boat, so they had to drag it behind.

'It's the Lord! It's Jesus!' the seven men began to whisper excitedly among themselves.

There was no stopping Peter. He leapt into the water and swam for the shore. The others followed in the boat, dragging the catch of fish behind them.

Reproduced with permission from *Stories to Read Aloud* published by BRF 2004 (1 84101 362 5)

'Bring some fish over here,' Jesus shouted as the lads reached the shore. 'I've got the barbecue going. Fish in a bun all round, with fries, yes?'

Everyone smiled and nodded.

Jesus and the seven men sat down to eat. Jesus deliberately sat next to Peter so that he could have a quiet word with him after breakfast.

'Tell me, Peter,' Jesus asked. 'Do you really love me as your friend?'

'Of course I do!' Peter replied.

There was a short silence before Jesus turned to Peter and spoke to him again.

'Are you sure, Peter?' Jesus quizzed.

'Of course I am!' Peter answered—a little put out this time. It reminded him of the way his father used to quiz him about things when he was a boy.

There was another short silence. Then Jesus turned to Peter again.

'Are you absolutely sure, Peter?' he asked.

Suddenly, Peter's memory was jogged. Jesus had asked him the question three times... and three times Peter had denied knowing Jesus, before the crucifixion. Peter began to feel a little shaky and very guilty.

'You know that I love you! You are my closest friend,' Peter replied, almost in tears. But he didn't know how to make things better.

'I know,' Jesus told him, smiling, 'but I wanted to hear you say it. I am going to give you another chance... there's lots of work to be done!'

Peter smiled a big smile. He was all ready to follow Jesus afresh and not let him down any more. It's a wonderful feeling to be given a second chance!

Reproduced with permission from *Stories to Read Aloud* published by BRF 2004 (1 84101 362 5)

Stories from the New Testament

— The book of Acts —

48

Receiving the Holy Spirit

Teacher's information

Bible reference

The story is based on Acts 1:12—2:41.

Theme

The Holy Spirit gives Jesus' friends power and special gifts with which to serve God.

Key verse

The Holy Spirit took control of everyone, and they began speaking in whatever languages the Spirit let them speak.
ACTS 2:4

Talk about…

The difficulties of telling our friends about Jesus.

Aim

To understand how the Holy Spirit equips people to live the Christian life and experience God in all his fullness.

Jigsaw puzzled

Dear God…
Can you help me to love others and tell them about Jesus?

Activitime

Have ready a small object and a glove. Ask what needs to be done if the small object is to be picked up using the glove. Then put your hand in the glove and do it—the job becomes easy. If the glove represents us, then what do the hand and the object to be picked up represent?

Jigsaw piece

After Jesus rose from the dead, and before he went back to his Father in heaven, he challenged his followers to continue his work on earth. He promised that they would receive the power to do it. The story of Pentecost sees that promise fulfilled.

Prayback

Almighty God,
*   Thank you that the Holy Spirit, like a hand within a glove, equips us to do the work of Jesus in the world today. Help us to love one another and to share the Christian message with those around us. In Jesus' name. Amen*

A gift from God

After Judas Iscariot, the person who had betrayed Jesus, had died, there were only eleven left of the original twelve men who had been Jesus' closest friends. Since Jesus had gone to heaven, they and his other followers had been doing a lot of praying.

'Do you think we should open a new church somewhere?' one of the lads asked at a meeting of the followers of Jesus. 'Or maybe run a children's club... or we could get together an outreach committee.'

'I think we should choose a replacement for Judas first,' Peter answered, 'and then we should keep on praying for God's guidance and power to help us continue the work of Jesus.'

There was a show of hands in response to the proposal and a man called Matthias was selected. Then everyone went on praying.

The days passed by. Knees got sore with the amount of kneeling in prayer that Jesus' followers were doing.

'What are we going to do today?' one of Jesus' close friends asked one morning.

There was no reply, just a smile from the others. He had known what the answer would be before he'd asked, so he rubbed his knees with ointment in preparation. Once again, as was their daily practice, the friends got down to praying. Little did they know that it was to be no ordinary day.

'Who's going to pray first?' one of the group asked.

There was a moment of silence, but once the praying started, it was a job to get a word in edgeways.

It happened to be a special festival day, so there were lots of people in Jerusalem from all sorts of different countries, making quite a lot of noise. It was a bit like being in the middle of a large international airport.

Suddenly, above the sound of footsteps and voices, there was a booming noise like a gale-force wind. People began to look up nervously, expecting to see dark storm clouds and torrential rain in the distance... but the sky was a clear blue. There was no rain and no wind, either.

'Very strange!'

'What's that peculiar noise?'

'In for a rough night,' people began to mutter.

Then suddenly, shouts of panic were heard above everything.

'Fire! Fire! That house is on fire!'

Sure enough, flames had appeared from nowhere, but nothing seemed to be burning.

The fire settled over the heads of Jesus' close friends as they prayed together in the house. But that wasn't all. As they began to

Reproduced with permission from *Stories to Read Aloud* published by BRF 2004 (1 84101 362 5)

speak, everyone in the crowd that had gathered outside the window heard them in their own language.

Some of the people were rather sceptical and thought that the men had been drinking.

'Someone's been to the Old Camel and Harp Inn,' they jeered.

Some thought that the friends had been to evening classes in languages. Others accepted it as the miracle that it was.

The noise like wind and the plumes of fire were just physical signs that the Holy Spirit had arrived. He had been sent by God to enable the followers of Jesus to continue his work on earth.

The fact that everyone present was able to hear Jesus' close friends' words in their own language was only part of the miracle of the Holy Spirit. The men were filled with the most amazing inner peace and joy. They felt full of the love of God, and each one was excited and eager to tell others about Jesus—with such confidence!

They rushed down to the crowded street. Peter stood with his friends and began to speak boldly. He preached to the amazed crowd about the events of the last few months—the cross, the resurrection and the ascension.

'He's a wonderful preacher,' people cried out.

There were shouts of 'I'm going to follow Jesus!' as people excitedly pushed to the front, to where the twelve men were standing. The eagerness, as people pushed and shoved, was like the New Year sales—and more! That day, three thousand people committed their lives to following Jesus.

'Now we are ready to build God's kingdom,' the friends said together.

They were confident that God had equipped them with all that they needed to live the Christian life and start his Church—thanks to the power of the Holy Spirit.

Reproduced with permission from *Stories to Read Aloud* published by BRF 2004 (1 84101 362 5)

49

Meeting with Jesus

Teacher's information

 ### Bible reference

The story is based on Acts 9:1–31.

 ### Theme

People are astonished at the change, for the better, in Saul since meeting with Jesus.

 ### Key verse

Everyone who heard Saul was amazed and said, 'Isn't this the man who caused so much trouble for those people in Jerusalem who worship in the name of Jesus? Didn't he come here to arrest them and take them to the chief priests?'
ACTS 9:21

Talk about...

Someone you would like to meet.

 ### Aim

To realize that meeting with Jesus changes lives, and it's something that we can all do.

Jigsaw puzzled

Dear God...
Does meeting with Jesus really make a difference?

 ### Activitime

Stain some paper, using cold tea or coffee, to make it look like an old piece of parchment. Write an imaginary letter from the high priest to the synagogues in Damascus, giving Saul the authority to arrest Christians there and take them back to Jerusalem.

 ### Jigsaw piece

After the ascension of Jesus into heaven, following his resurrection, we read about the growth of the Christian Church. In the early days, there was much opposition to Christians and many of them were tortured and killed. This is a story of a man who is on his way to persecute followers of Jesus, but something amazing happens before he reaches his destination.

Prayback

Lord Jesus,
We thank you that you were able to transform Saul's life for the better when he met with you on the road to Damascus. We thank you that you still transform people's lives when they meet with you today. Please help those who haven't yet met you in a personal way to do so. Amen

A dazzling experience

Saul might have been a nice person to know if you were a Pharisee, but certainly not if you were a Christian. You see, Saul hated Christians, and it had become his life's ambition to arrest and persecute as many as he could. He believed that he was doing it for the good of the established religion and ultimately for God—but of course he wasn't.

Anyway, one day, Saul was travelling to Damascus.

'Let me at those troublesome Christians,' he growled to the others travelling with him, sounding like an angry bear. 'The sooner we've done away with all of them, the better.'

'Down with Christians!' they all shouted together, with bloodcurdling devotion to the cause. They began to laugh in a very sinister manner.

'Hurry up!' Saul shouted as he walked out in front, eager to get on with the job—but not for long!

Suddenly, an incredibly dazzling light shone down from the sky on to Saul. It was so bright that it seemed to shine right through him. It was like being caught in the beam of a really bright spotlight on stage—but brighter!

Saul fell to the ground, dazzled and terrified. Then he heard a voice that seemed to come from nowhere. It was rather creepy.

'Saul, why are you doing this to me?' the voice demanded, like a disappointed parent.

Saul wasn't so bold now, I can tell you. He curled up into a little ball on the road, rather like a scared hedgehog. In between pleas for his life, he asked who the mystery voice belonged to.

'It's me,' the voice replied. 'Jesus. The one you are persecuting.'

Saul's knees began to knock, and sweat poured from his brow. He had been sure that Jesus was dead and out of the way, and now he'd come to get his own back—or so Saul thought!

But Jesus hadn't come to harm Saul. He just wanted him to preach the Christian message all over the world—no small task!

'Go to Damascus, and you will be told what you must do,' Jesus instructed him.

With that, the bright light disappeared and

all was quiet. Saul began to move slowly and nervously, in case there were any more surprises.

Saul's colleagues, who hadn't understood what had happened, ran over to him as he picked himself up from the ground.

'That must have been some strong stuff you were drinking in Jerusalem last night,' they laughed. 'If we'd known, we'd have had some as well!'

'I can't see!' Saul shouted, frozen to the spot like a frightened rabbit caught in a car's headlights. 'I can't see!'

By this time, the others were rather worried but, despite that, they helped Saul along the road to Damascus—where he remained blind for three days.

On the third day, a man called Ananias arrived. God had spoken to him in a kind of dream. He was a Christian, so, as you can imagine, he hadn't been very enthusiastic about visiting Saul—the persecutor of Christians.

'I'm too young to die!' Ananias had moaned.

'I know what you're saying,' God had replied, 'but trust me—it will be all right. I have chosen Saul to teach people about me.'

So Ananias went and placed his hands on Saul's eyes, and Saul was able to see again. Saul was overjoyed. What's more, the whole experience had a very lasting effect on him. As a result, he decided to follow Jesus.

I don't need to tell you that, for a time, Saul was viewed with great suspicion by other Christians. Despite that, he went on to do all sorts of wonderful things in the early Christian Church. He spread the good news about Jesus far and wide.

In fact, it has to be said that the day when Saul met Jesus face to face, and committed his life to following him, was a very special day— one that Saul would never forget. And Saul marked the wonderful change that had taken place in his life by changing his name to 'Paul'.

Reproduced with permission from *Stories to Read Aloud* published by BRF 2004 (1 84101 362 5)

50

God can use even 'bad times' for good

Teacher's information

 Bible reference

The story is based on Acts 16:16–40.

 Theme

Paul and Silas make the best of a bad situation, by spending time singing hymns and praying.

 Key verse

About midnight Paul and Silas were praying and singing praises to God, while the other prisoners listened.
ACTS 16:25

 Talk about...

What it means to make the best of a bad situation.

 Aim

To ask God to use all the situations we find ourselves in, for good.

Jigsaw puzzled

Dear God...
Can anything good come out of bad situations?

 Activitime

Two volunteers are needed. They should sit on two chairs at the front and imagine that they are in an ancient prison. Conditions are bad, there is no food and they are chained to the wall. Make up a dialogue concerning what is 'good' about being a prisoner (it may be humorous).

 Jigsaw piece

After his conversion, Paul spent a lot of his time going around from place to place, telling people about Jesus. On one of these trips, together with his friend Silas, Paul drove an evil spirit out of a slave girl who had been earning a lot of money telling fortunes. Freed from the evil spirit, she lost the ability to earn money in that way. Her master was not pleased. After the resulting disturbance, Paul and Silas are arrested, flogged and put into prison.

Prayback

Faithful heavenly Father,
Thank you for your love for us in all situations. Please help us to praise you even in the hard times, like Paul and Silas did, and inspire us to allow you to bring something good and positive out of even the most difficult experiences that we have to go through. In Jesus' name. Amen

What shall we do next?

Having been stripped and flogged, Paul and Silas were dragged into the dark, damp prison cell. The smell was appalling—like a mixture of rotten eggs and old trainers. As the prison officer was putting Paul's and Silas' feet into the stocks, one of the other prisoners was swearing and cursing, others had just given up on life and some were squabbling to pass the time.

'I spy with my little eye… something beginning with B.'

'Bars.'

'Yes.'

'I spy with my little eye… something beginning with C.'

'Chains.'

'Yes.'

'Oh, this is so boring. We've done all these before!'

'Well, there's not much choice in a place like this, is there?'

'If I wasn't chained up, I'd thump you.'

And so the trivial arguments went on!

Paul and Silas listened in despair to the shouting, the negative attitudes and the bickering.

'Let's sing a song,' Paul suggested, putting on a brave face.

Silas nodded in agreement. 'What shall we sing, then?' he asked.

Paul broke into song with one of their favourite hymns, and Silas joined in.

'I feel better already,' Paul commented when they had finished.

'Let's have another,' Silas said, and began to sing again.

The prisoners looked on, stunned. They had never seen anyone behave like that in prison before. Then Paul began to pray.

'Lord, we praise you for this wonderful time of fellowship together,' he said. 'It's good to have a break from the busyness of the day, to spend time with you.'

Silas joined in, praising God for his goodness to them.

By this time, it was the middle of the night. Suddenly, the ground began to move as a mighty earthquake shook the prison. It was so violent that all the doors flew open and everybody's chains broke loose. For the prisoners, it was like a dream come true.

'Let's go, lads,' one of them shouted excitedly.

'No!' Paul commanded, with such authority that no one moved. He sounded just like a head teacher.

⚶

When the jailer woke up, he thought that all the prisoners had escaped. For him, such failure in his duties would have meant punishment by death. He panicked and, in despair, was about to kill himself when Paul shouted out.

'Don't do it! We're still here!'

The jailer couldn't believe it. He immediately invited Paul and Silas into his house, and, after washing their wounds, the jailer and all his family listened to the message of Jesus.

'I want to give my life to Jesus and be baptized!' the jailer shouted joyfully.

And all his family followed. What a night!

⚶

Next day, when Paul and Silas were released, they turned to each other, smiling, and said, 'If we hadn't got arrested, none of these people would have given their lives to Jesus.'

God constantly surprises us by bringing good out of the most difficult situations, when we follow Jesus.

Reproduced with permission from *Stories to Read Aloud* published by BRF 2004 (1 84101 362 5)